Page 100

JAN 1972

FRANKLIN D. ROOSEVELT

Portrait of a President

by JOSEPH GIES

1971
DOUBLEDAY & COMPANY, INC.
Garden City, New York

6845

PRINTED IN THE UNITED STATES OF AMERICA

Contents

Acknowledgment

THE PREPARATION of this book would have been impossible without the intelligent and helpful co-operation of the personnel at the Franklin D. Roosevelt Library—Director James O'Neill, Acting Director William J. Stewart, Paul McLaughlin, Joseph Marshall, and their associates.

The staff made available the library's extensive collection of Roosevelt photographs, enabling many rarely seen pictures to be included in this book. In fact, unless otherwise indicated next to the picture, all photographs are from the files of the Franklin D. Roosevelt Library and are used with their permission.

J.G.

Franklin D. Roosevelt
Portrait of a President

1

Sara's Boy

THE ten-pound baby born to Sara Delano Roosevelt at Springwood, Hyde Park, New York, on January 30, 1882, came into
the world with all the advantages a boy could ask for. His parents
were almost as rich as their neighbors the Vanderbilts, and one
drawer higher in social standing. A dozen of his Delano ancestors
had crowded aboard the *Mayflower,* making Sara the leading gen-
ealogical bore of the Hudson Valley. The baby's father, James
Roosevelt, was descended from a succession of New Amsterdam
businessmen named van Rosenvelt who had democratized their
patronym at the time of the American Revolution. Though James's
more daring speculations, aimed at partnership in major robber-
baron monopolies, missed fire, he did very well with the Delaware
& Hudson Canal Company, which dealt in anthracite coal, while
Sara eventually inherited a million dollars, largely the fruit of Warren
Delano's opium operations in Hong Kong during the Civil War.

James was a fifty-two-year-old widower when he married Sara,
a beauty of twenty-six who had turned down a number of younger
suitors. The baby, named Franklin Delano after two months of
pondering, was an only child. He was spoiled, but not badly. The
dresses and kilts he wore till he rebelled at the age of eight were
carefully bundled up, labeled, and saved. Sara did not anticipate
that her son would be President; she thought his ancestry guaranteed
that posterity would be interested. Franklin was taken on his first
European trip when he was three, and thereafter nearly every year.
In the woods back of Springwood he hunted and rode his pony.
He collected birds with a gun and learned to stuff them himself.

1

Franklin and his mother, Sara, 1882

*Springwood, the Roosevelts' Hyde Park home
as it looked in 1900*

Summers he went fishing on the Hudson, winters ice-boating. At six he began private lessons with the neighboring Rogers children, whose father was a Rockefeller aide. His first teacher was a German lady, his second French. He enjoyed reading, especially boys' adventure stories—Kipling was about as deep as his reading ever got—and eventually became a book collector. But the summer he was nine his father bought a 51-foot sailboat, the *Half Moon,* and from then on books took second place. They sailed the *Half Moon* in the Hudson and up at Campobello Island, New Brunswick, opposite the tiptop of Maine, where James Roosevelt had built a comfortable cottage.

James had graduated from little Union College and afterward attended Harvard Law School. Franklin was pointed toward Harvard by way of a new but fashionable boarding school at Groton, Massachusetts, founded by the earnest, idealistic son of a Morgan partner, the Reverend Endicott Peabody. Groton was a barefaced copy of the English boys' school, even to a fives court. However, the Reverend Peabody stopped short of the barbarous corporal

Franklin poses for a photograph taken during his first trip to Europe at the age of three.

James and Franklin Roosevelt, June 1883. The two were close companions during Franklin's boyhood.

punishments of the English schools, limiting himself to solemn reprimands in the Rector's study.

Because Sara was reluctant to part with him, Franklin was a couple of years past the normal age for an entering boy, but he fitted into Groton so smoothly as to indicate a distinct talent for adaptation. Finding his accent not quite right for Boston-oriented Groton, he broadened his *a* and suppressed his *r*. In class he avoided all black marks until he discovered that a certain number were considered a sign of "school spirit," whereupon he took care to acquire a few. He was never in peril of the "pump" or the "boot box," forms of torture occasionally used by the older boys on uppity juniors. He achieved few academic distinctions—gentlemen by tradition were mediocre students. In his last year he was a prefect (dormitory proctor) and manager of the baseball team, the latter post one whose status Sara happily exaggerated.

In the spring of 1898 heady events in the outside world impinged on Groton. Franklin Roosevelt and two schoolmates plotted to run off to Boston and join the Navy, but a scarlet fever epidemic

3

Franklin and Sara Delano Roosevelt
in 1893

James and Sara Roosevelt at St. Blasien,
Baden, August 25, 1896. Taken by F.D.R.

F.D.R. and his cousins visit Grandfather Delano at Fairhaven,
Massachusetts, September 1897.

frustrated the plan. Hastening home from Europe, Sara circumvented quarantine by climbing a precarious ladder outside the infirmary window several times a day to check on her convalescent.

Meantime the Navy covered itself with facile glory in Manila Bay and Cuba without his aid, while an older Roosevelt charged to the front of the political scene in his Rough Rider image. Teddy was so remote a cousin as to be virtually unrelated (he even pronounced his name differently—"Rews" instead of "Rose"), but Franklin was an enthusiastic admirer, as were all his Groton schoolmates and all right-thinking American boys everywhere.

At his graduation Franklin surprised everyone, including himself, by carrying off the Latin prize, a set of Shakespeare. On that note of unexpected triumph he went off to Campobello for a summer of sailing before enrolling at Harvard in the fall of 1900.

At Harvard, rich men's sons from Boston and New York segregated themselves in clubs and concentrated on perfecting their status etiquette, while bright middle-class boys from places like Buffalo hung on the words of William James, George Santayana, and Josiah Royce. Roosevelt of course belonged to the former group. His first act on moving into his three-room apartment on Mt. Auburn Street was to send home for his pipe, indispensable symbol of the young man who went to college not to learn, though he could not smoke it because he was out for freshman football.

Lack of poundage on his gangling six-foot-two frame balked football success, but he did a lot of grunting and sweating in the spirit of T.R. In his sophomore year he was hazed into DKE and the Institute of 1770—"My back is a bit raw, but I am through the first ordeal O.K.," he wrote home—and later became a member of the Fly Club and Hasty Pudding. His marks were properly undistinguished, but he worked hard, earning his degree in three years in order to devote his fourth year exclusively to the *Harvard Crimson.* By toil and enterprise he rose to competition with two classmates for the top editorial job, called for some reason "president," and won, assuming his post in the autumn of 1903.

As head of the *Crimson,* he conducted a succession of crusades. Aided by Prexy Eliot's slip into the mire, he got more duckboards put on the campus walks in bad weather. Even more worthwhile, he drew attention to the shortage of fire escapes on dormitories and classroom buildings. But true to the Siwash era tradition, he devoted his editorial attention principally to sports, especially football. Applying a splendid combination of ingenuity and determination, he scooped the *Yale Daily News* in its own backyard by getting a *Crimson* extra with the score of the Harvard-Yale game hawked

5

F.D.R. as a member of Groton's fourth-string football team (center)

Franklin as Uncle Bopaddy (right) in the Groton school play, "The Wedding March," February 22, 1900

Father and son at Groton, April 1899

The house at Campobello

*During Franklin's youth, at least part of
each summer was spent at Campobello.*

F.D.R. with Tip at Campobello

The Half Moon II *under full sail at Campobello*

Franklin takes James and Helen Roosevelt out on his first yacht, the New Moon.

to the crowd coming out of the Yale Bowl. But he reacted humorlessly to the game in which the Carlisle Indian boys beat Harvard by stuffing a football up the back of a jersey. The *Crimson* advocated as a corrective to the team's difficulties "a spirit of aggressive, vigorous determination."

Though he enrolled at Columbia Law School the following autumn to acquire the requisites for a career, Roosevelt's liberal education ended with Harvard. By American educational standards of a later day (whatever *their* shortcomings) the store of knowledge he took

8

away from Harvard was unimpressive. His history was mainly political, distinctly militarist, and filled with racist implications. His economics was based on an unrealistic theoretical model of capitalism, rendered absurd by the rise of the giant trusts—A.T.&T., Standard Oil, U.S. Steel. His picture of the world's art and literature was distorted in favor of the West, especially England. His science was limited to a little geology, giving him scant awareness of the revolution in chemistry and physics that was beginning to unlock the secrets of the universe.

Eleanor with her father, Elliott, and brothers Hall and Ellie

A new year and a new century are celebrated at Hyde Park.

THE BETTMANN ARCHIVE

With the staff of the Harvard Crimson, *1902* (*2nd row center*)

A Harvard man, 1903

F.D.R. hams it up at Steen Valetje, home of his uncle Warren Delano at Barrytown, New York, 1902.

10

The Anglo-American 1900's had a phrase, "ladies' man," which carried the oddly mixed connotation of Don Juanism and effeminacy. Franklin Roosevelt was not reputed a ladies' man. He squired girls, he did not chase them. Consequently Sara was startled by the news that at twenty-two he had fallen madly in love and wanted to get married. The girl was certainly suitable—nineteen-year-old Eleanor Roosevelt (fifth cousin once removed) was a little homely, but she made up for that with a tall, willowy figure and a lively personality. She had the innocence of a proper rich girl and an appealing modesty, the remnant of a childhood inferiority complex. Eleanor's family was a high-class cast of *You Can't Take It With You:* Mother

The newly engaged couple during a visit to Campobello, 1904

Sara and Eleanor at Campobello

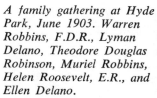

A family gathering at Hyde Park, June 1903. Warren Robbins, F.D.R., Lyman Delano, Theodore Douglas Robinson, Muriel Robbins, Helen Roosevelt, E.R., and Ellen Delano.

Members of the wedding party of Helen Roosevelt and
Theodore Douglas Robinson, Hyde Park, June 18, 1904

Anna Hall Roosevelt had been a spoiled beauty; father Elliott a gentlemanly alcoholic who spent much of his time at a fashionable drying-out farm, Uncles Vallie and Eddie Hall just a few bottles behind him; Aunt Pussie was a fountain of Fifth Avenue scandal. Among her mother's family, the Halls, were also an assortment of admirals, diplomats, and tycoons. But everything else Eleanor had in the way of kinfolk was put in the shade by Uncle Teddy, the violently charismatic President of the United States. Whatever ice that cut with Sara, it must have cut a little with Franklin.

Eleanor had surprising sophistication in an area about which Edwardian girls were supposed to know no more than they were supposed to know about sex. A little French lady named Mlle. Souvestre who ran a girls' boarding school in England had intro-

Mrs. Franklin Roosevelt, March 17, 1905

duced Eleanor to the strong new wine of social justice—the idea
that something actually could be done about the vast junk heaps of
human misery with which laissez-faire had strewn the landscape.
While Franklin was exhorting Harvard undergraduates to cheer
harder, Eleanor was climbing stairs in the New York garment dis-

trict, and discovering that dress manufacturers did not believe in investing needlessly in ladies' rooms or fire escapes.

This element of Eleanor's personality did not appeal to Sara, who found social reform an inappropriate interest for a multiple descendant of the *Mayflower*. She took Franklin off on a West Indies cruise to forget. He didn't. "Franklin's feelings did not change," Eleanor recorded with satisfaction, long years after. In the fall of 1904 the engagement was announced, and at Thanksgiving Eleanor was at last invited into the bosom of the family—Sara's family, the Delanos—at Fairhaven, Massachusetts. Over the door hung the coat of arms of "Jehan de Lannoy, Knight of the Golden Fleece" and forebear of Philippe de Lannoy, who arrived in North America a little tardily, in 1621, but who made up for that by being a genuine 14-karat aristocrat, putting the Delanos one up on even their *Mayflower* steerage mates.

But at the wedding the Delanos had to take second place. The date was March 17 (1905), chosen because Uncle Teddy was coming to New York to review the St. Patrick's Day parade. The wedding was held in two adjoining houses on East 76th Street belonging to two of Eleanor's relatives. Seventy-five policemen held back the crowds as the President gave away his niece who, everybody noticed, was taller than he was. The earnest Reverend Peabody came down from Groton to perform the ceremony and share the prestige.

Afterwards, the bride and groom turned to receive the felicitations of their friends, but found themselves alone—everybody had followed Uncle Ted into the library. Docilely, the young couple did the same. T.R. regaled the crowd with a few stories and left. Anticlimactically, so did Franklin and Eleanor.

14

2

A Snob in Politics

FITTING the wedding into Teddy Roosevelt's schedule upset the honeymoon arrangements. They spent a week at the Hyde Park house, then moved into a hotel while Franklin finished the spring term at Columbia. Since Eleanor's training had protected her from such plebeian accomplishments as cooking, a hotel was more practical than an apartment. In June they took a real honeymoon befitting their station—three months in Europe. They dined, shopped, sightsaw, and photographed in a ritual already established by rich English and American couples. In Venice, Franklin snapped Eleanor's picture primly reclining in a gondola, holding her husband's straw hat. They worried about having enough money when Brown's Hotel in London insisted on putting them in the royal suite—and even more about having the right clothes. Eleanor was shocked by the bathing suits on the Lido and "suffered tortures" at an English country estate where they played bridge for money, something both contrary to her principles and outside her talents. But the grand tour was fun, and they returned home with Eleanor pregnant.

On their arrival in New York, Sara Roosevelt took charge. She moved them into a house on 36th Street, three blocks from her own, redecorated according to her taste, supplied with servants picked by her. This arrangement was temporary, until Sara could build two adjoining brownstones further uptown, on 65th Street. In furnishing the house assigned to Franklin and Eleanor, Sara consulted Franklin but not Eleanor, who burst into a fit of weeping one night at the sight of the dressing table her mother-in-law had

*Franklin and Eleanor at Algonac,
the Delano family estate at
Newburgh, New York, May 7, 1905*

selected for her. Gently and reasonably Franklin reproved her. Eleanor got hold of herself and resolved to master the difficulties of marriage to an only son. Aware that she was no sailor, she tried golf, his second favorite sport, but after a couple of rounds he kindly advised her to forget that too. She had not yet found her real connection to this happy, confident, bright young husband, but she did not give up trying.

He himself was groping for something. He dropped out of law school as soon as he passed his bar exam (1907), without waiting to get a degree. Yet the job he took was bland—junior clerk for a Wall Street firm called Carter, Ledyard & Milburn. First year no salary, next few years a very small one, but then a junior partnership and so on up—a career program calculated to attract rich young men and turn them into rich old men. Carter, Ledyard specialized in defending the big, new, buccaneering corporations like Standard Oil and American Tobacco against anti-trust suits by Teddy Roosevelt's aggressive Department of Justice. Franklin did not get personally involved in this glamour branch of the business. As clerk in charge of "municipal cases" he defended the firm's corporate clients against petty suits by customers who claimed they had been cheated. Often he settled out of court with an opposing lawyer working on a percentage basis. The dingy courtrooms, the sorry litigants, and the shyster lawyers might have provided a disagreeable experience for a young man from a merely middle-class background. For Roosevelt they were an illuminating novelty, a taste of real life.

16

Eleanor's aunt, Mrs. Stanley Mortimer, and her children joined the honeymooners at St. Moritz, Switzerland.

n route to Fontainebleau. With Eleanor and F.D.R. are Mr. and Mrs. William Forbes (Eleanor's aunt) nd Franklin's cousin, Warren Robbins.

Just as the small salary he began to receive at the end of his first year was a pledge of the comfortable income Wall Street promised, so several small-claims cases his relatives threw his way were a harbinger of the important clients a Roosevelt might be expected to attract to the firm. He could look forward very securely to a lifetime of pleasant work, weekends at Hyde Park, sailing in the summer, trips to Europe. To Sara the prospect was pleasing, and Eleanor was still too modest to have an opinion. But it left Franklin cold. He was drawn to Washington, where Uncle Teddy lighted up the sky like an electric sign. When Eleanor's beautiful cousin Alice Roosevelt wed Speaker of the House Nicholas Longworth, pregnant Eleanor could not attend, but in-law Franklin went. Uncle Teddy told him public service was a duty of the elite, and Franklin listened to the sermon with pleasure.

What he wanted was an opportunity to put Uncle Teddy's recommendation into practice. It did not come quickly. But in 1910, after three years on Wall Street, he received a visit from a Dutchess County Democratic leader. The Hyde Park Roosevelts were Democrats—conservative, or "gold" Democrats in the terminology of James Roosevelt's day. The local Dutchess County state assemblyman, Lewis Stuyvesant Chanler, was a wealthy, aristocratic, middle-aged politico who had already run for governor; it seemed likely that he would lay aside the cares of office at the next election. The party was looking around for a younger man in the same pattern—that is, a well-fixed socialite who could pay for his own campaign and contribute to the party besides. If his name happened to be Roosevelt, that was frosting on the cake.

To Sara's dismay, the twenty-eight-year-old law clerk jumped at the bait. Presented to the party leaders at a clambake, he made a good enough impression, despite a few reservations over his political inexperience and his social maladdress—the Groton-Harvard posture didn't fit a Poughkeepsie clambake. Then somebody found out that Chanler did not mean to retire after all. Roosevelt took the older man out to dinner and proposed that he run for the more prestigious post of state senator. Chanler wasn't having any of that—the assembly district, mostly Poughkeepsie, was Democratic, but the larger senate district was Republican. Chanler turned the argument around—why didn't Roosevelt run for the senate? The pro politicians, having trouble finding somebody who could afford to run for the senate, added their pressure.

Roosevelt asked for twenty-four hours to think it over. Given his natural optimism and the tantalizing whiff of politics, the outcome was foregone. Dedicating himself to independence from the bosses

The Roosevelts' first home, at 125 East 36th Street

At Strathpeffer, Scotland

F.D.R. photographed Eleanor and the gondolier in Venice.

Franklin with Eleanor on the steps at Hyde Park, 1906

and "good government," he promised a "very strenuous campaign" —clichés borrowed from Uncle Teddy, which he meant, especially the strenuous campaign. His most important decision was to take politicking out of the horse-and-buggy age. There was only one suitable automobile to be had, but it was a great one—a big open Maxwell, painted red, with brass headlamps and no top or windshield. Festooning it with flags and bunting, he hit the trail. There were few crowds. Mostly he talked to people face to face, striding into the general store with hand stuck out, pulling into the farmyard to hail farmers (or their wives, even though women didn't vote yet in New York), stopping sweaty teamsters on the dirt roads and inviting them to call him by his first name. When he did address a group he hit on a nice opening: "My friends . . ." (somehow nobody has quite topped that one yet).

Despite sidestepping party politics and issues, he worked with the party, contributing a healthy $2500 to the local campaign fund and taking in return all the help he could get. The Democratic Congres-

20

sional candidate, Richard Connell, an old campaigner who knew the district backwards, traveled many miles in the Maxwell with him, giving invaluable tips. It was Connell who taught him to establish a bond with an audience by first saying something about the town or the district before bringing up politics.

He wasn't very smooth—"I know I am no orator," he told them truthfully. "You don't have to be an orator, Roosevelt," a farmer called out. He attacked the bosses of both parties—the local Republican boss who was unpopular with the farmers, and of course Tammany. He unblushingly exploited his name, with frequent use of the T.R. word "bully." T.R., back from an African safari, was shaking up the Republican party with his exasperation over his Presidential successor, massive William Howard Taft, whom he had picked himself.

With Eleanor, Anna, and Duffy at Campobello, 1907

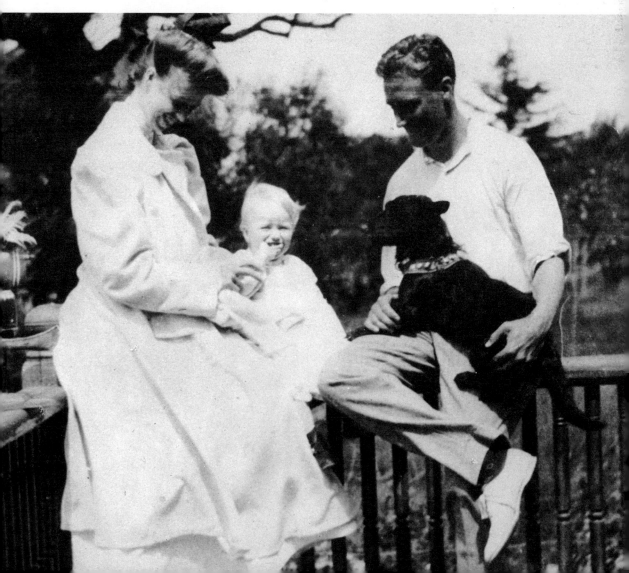

F.D.R. enjoyed the same warm relationship with his children that he and his father had shared. Above, with Elliott at Campobello. Below, with Anna.

Awaking at the last minute to the danger posed by the Democratic Roosevelt, the local Republican press made an effort to hang his Wall Street affiliation on him—Carter, Ledyard was at that very moment defending the hated Sugar Trust against government prosecution. But it was too late to bring that up. On election day he ran way out in front of the ticket, carrying Dutchess County by 1140, nearly 500 ahead of the victorious Democratic candidate for governor.

It was a triumphant beginning, and it was immediately clear that it was only a beginning. While most of his fellow legislators moved frugally into hotel rooms and boarding houses for the session, the twenty-nine-year-old squire of Hyde Park rented a commodious house on State Street for his growing family—Eleanor, four-year-old Anna, three-year-old Jimmy, and baby Elliott, accompanied by a retinue of nurses and servants. When the session erupted in a battle over the U.S. senatorship (legislatures still picked U.S. senators) the State Street house became headquarters for anti-Tammany Democrats plotting to upset Boss Murphy's choice, a traction magnate named "Blue-Eyed Billy" Sheehan. The noisy, convivial, cigar-smoking crowd alarmed and half-asphyxiated Eleanor, who bravely served refreshments at midnight and hinted that everybody should go home.

But the fight against Tammany, eventually settled by the inevitable compromise, did Roosevelt enormous good. He emerged from it as a "progressive leader," his name mentioned in newspapers across the country. Throughout the remainder of the session he strengthened, or at least guarded, that reputation by backing a bill to limit factory labor by boys to fifty-four hours a week, and did not oppose woman suffrage, though he was too cautious to come right out and say women should vote.

If he didn't already know it, Roosevelt learned quickly that caution was an important part of a politician's armament. One of his fellow-insurgents in the Blue-Eyed Billy Sheehan affair ran a country newspaper and depended on state printing jobs to keep going. Boss Murphy had his contract canceled and drove him into bankruptcy.

Tammany played rough. Yet a starry-eyed young alumna of Mount Holyoke and Jane Addams' Hull House demonstrated another side of bossism. A busy lobbyist for do-good legislation, Frances Perkins found Franklin Roosevelt at first less responsive than a couple of young Tammany leaders in the legislature—Bob Wagner and Al Smith. Up from the city streets, Wagner and Smith had a knowledge of gritty social realities that people like Franklin and Eleanor Roosevelt had to acquire. Eleanor had already begun with Mlle. Souvestre; through Frances Perkins, Franklin got started. When a hundred and fifty girls were suffocated in a Seventh Avenue loft with

23

Sporting with Frances de Rham, wife of one of F.D.R.'s Harvard classmates, and cousin Laura Delano. Campobello, about 1910.

Eleanor sailing at Campobello, about 1908

only one fire escape, major pioneering factory legislation was launched in Albany by Frances Perkins, Al Smith, Bob Wagner, and even Boss Murphy, who found that social legislation paid off in votes.

Watching Wagner and Smith buttonhole delegates in the cloakroom and the hotel bars, Roosevelt began to get the hang of mixing with the hoi polloi. "Awfully arrogant fellow, that Roosevelt," one old Tammany Irishman complained to Frances Perkins. He wasn't, really. He had to change his style from Groton-Harvard, but he didn't have to change his attitude. He could adapt to other people because, basically, he liked them.

Back in Groton days he had bought a couple of pairs of glasses, and decided he liked the pince-nez. The fact that the ribboned spectacles gave him a snob image did not bother him, because he knew he

Anna, Sara, and Eleanor enjoy a sail at Campobello.

was no snob. Instead of discarding the pince-nez when he went into politics he made it a trademark, and in the end won acceptance.

When Uncle Teddy, robbed of the Republican nomination by the party bosses, split the GOP in 1912 with his Bull Moose movement, hopeful Democrats all over the country jumped to take advantage. Roosevelt quickly spotted Woodrow Wilson, professorial governor of New Jersey, as the rising star of reform Democrats, and helped start a Wilson organization in upstate New York. Boss Murphy supported conservative Champ Clark of Missouri (who had a great song, "You Gotta Quit Kickin' My Dog Around," but not much else) and coolly shut Roosevelt and his crowd out of the New York delegation to the Baltimore convention. Roosevelt went anyway and made himself briefly conspicuous by leading a floor demonstration for Wilson.

25

A candidate for the state senate campaigns in Dutchess County, 1910. Eleanor stands behind her husband.

The support of William Jennings Bryan was a more substantial aid to Wilson, who after 46 ballots and plenty of wheeling and dealing, got the nomination.

Still, Roosevelt had identified himself prominently with the winner, and Wilson counted on him to help carry New York. He planned a vigorous campaign both in Wilson's behalf and his own, but a terrible stroke of luck suddenly threatened to cost him his state senate seat and perhaps his political future. He caught typhoid fever, and was confined to bed for the whole campaign. In this critical dilemma he thought of Louis McHenry Howe.

Howe was a typical newspaperman—smart, underpaid, frustrated, on the lookout for a buck, and fascinated by politics. His father had come home from the Civil War to make money as a banker in Indianapolis, lose it in the Panic of '73, clutch at kinfolk's help in Saratoga Springs, and fight for recovery of self-respect with a weekly newspaper. Louis Howe grew up in the printing shop, landed stringer jobs with New York papers in Saratoga during the racing season and in Albany during the legislative session. A Democrat by family conviction, he had made Franklin Roosevelt the hero of his reports on the Blue-Eyed Billy Sheehan fight. In return Roosevelt had thrown some public relations work Howe's way in the upstate Wilson-for-President campaign.

Small, frail, his face pitted by a bicycle accident, Howe sardonically called himself "one of the four homeliest men in the state of

*In his state senate campaign, F.D.R. generally neglected
the safe Democratic districts and wooed the rural areas.*

Eleanor with James, Elliott, and Anna, June 1911

New York." Eleanor Roosevelt, put off by his slovenly appearance and cigarette addiction, badly underestimated the little gnome. For a $50-a-week salary, Howe took immediate, complete, and professional charge of Roosevelt's 1912 campaign. Cynical, inventive, and indefatigable, he wrote direct-mail copy and sent it to Roosevelt with the note, "Here is your first ad. . . . As I have pledged you in it I thought you might like to know what kind of mess I was getting you into. Please *wire* o.k. . . . Your friend the city clerk is going to have a list of every member of the Grange for me tomorrow. . . ." He jotted a stream of notes on promises he had made—"(a job) at $2,500 or more," a "Coat Room Attendant," a "State Fair Commissioner," a printing contract. He lent Roosevelt's car "to tote the archbishop up from Fishkill" and help scotch a rumor that Roosevelt was anti-Catholic. He even turned Roosevelt's illness into an asset, picturing the invalid busily dictating campaign material from his sick bed while his lackadaisical rival loafed. Organizing a "Franklin D. Roosevelt Club," he distributed two hundred $5 checks to election workers on election day. Howe's results were spectacular—victory by over 1600 votes.

Roosevelt discovered Howe, and Howe discovered Roosevelt. The combination was perfect.

On his feet again, Roosevelt promoted a series of bills to help New York farmers, enlisting the co-operation of an expert, Liberty Hyde Bailey of the State Agricultural College at Cornell. Maneuvering skillfully, not disdaining to compromise, using Louis Howe to build a farmers' counter-lobby to the lobby of the processors, Roosevelt got his bills passed.

That victory marked his arrival as a mature politician on the state level. By the time it was finally won he had moved up to the national stage.

F.D.R. at the helm, having tea with Sara; his aunt Frances Hitch; H. S. Hooker, one of his closest friends; and Eleanor. Campobello, 1911.

F.D.R. in his state senate seat in Albany

Consulted by Wilson on patronage for upstate New York Democrats, he was not the man to turn coy when his own name came up. He was offered his choice of two glamour appointments, an assistant secretaryship in either Treasury or Navy. Treasury, headed in the new administration by William Gibbs McAdoo, was the more prestigious department, but Navy had only one assistant, and besides, it was the very office Uncle Teddy had held, and besides that, he was a sailor, not an accountant.

Wilson's Secretary of the Navy was a deceptively simple country editor from North Carolina named Josephus Daniels. On Inauguration Day he buttonholed Roosevelt in the lobby of the Willard and made the formal offer. How would he like to be Assistant Secretary of the Navy? "I'd like it bully well!" beamed T.R.'s distant cousin and nephew-by-marriage.

Kidding with the newspapermen a couple of days later, he reminded them of what had happened "the last time a Roosevelt sat at this desk." Uncle Teddy had taken advantage of an absent chief to order Dewey to prepare an attack on Manila Bay, two months before war was declared.

Franklin Roosevelt had no such plans, and no more anticipation of coming war than anyone else in Washington. But he was well aware that he had taken a big step up the political ladder, and he meant to make the most of the opportunity.

30

3

Battleships and Ballots

THE ROOSEVELTS moved into Washington the same way they had
moved into Albany—as if they owned the town. While U.S.
senators crowded their families into apartment hotels, the Roosevelt limousine drew up before one of the capital's better-known resi-
dences, a commodious house at 1733 N Street. The place belonged
to Eleanor's Auntie Bye, and had once served as temporary White
House while T.R. waited for Mrs. McKinley to clear out of 1600
Pennsylvania Avenue. Two servants and a gardener went with it;
from Albany and New York the Roosevelts brought more, including
a chauffeur to ferry Eleanor on the stupefying round of social calls
imposed by Washington's leaden protocol—Monday the wives of
Supreme Court justices received, Tuesday the wives of congressmen,
and on through the week. Only on weekends was there time to relax.
Franklin played thirty-six holes of golf and took the children to see
the model ships in the Navy Department. He fenced at the new
Fencing Club organized by Colonel Robert M. Thompson, the
wealthy president of the Navy League. They dined, partied, and
danced—the tango was the hot new step—though Eleanor had to
limit her dancing in 1913–14, when she was pregnant for the fifth
time. One child, named Franklin, Jr., had died at Hyde Park; the new
baby was also named Franklin, Jr. (Their fifth and last child, John,
was born in 1916.)

Sundays they had a few friends in for supper. Among these were
the Franklin Lanes, and Eleanor was still rather surprised to recall
thirty years later that the Sunday night party was so informal that
Lane, Secretary of the Interior, did not have to be seated "according
to his rank." Herbert and Lou Hoover, a pleasant couple from

31

With Theodore Douglas Robinson in front of the State, Army and Navy Building, Washington

F.D.R. in New York to lay the keel of ₩39, March 16, 1914. Senator O'Gorman is on his left.

California, were often present. Roosevelt esteemed the capable food administrator, and wrote a friend, "I wish we could make him President of the United States." Eleanor scrambled eggs in a chafing dish to go with cold cuts from the delicatessen.

Washington was fun, but Roosevelt did not originally intend to be there long. Uncle Teddy had resigned from the Navy Department after two years to make the charge up San Juan Hill to the State House in Albany. In 1913 there was no San Juan Hill in sight, but the New York governorship and one senatorship were coming up for grabs the next year. That was why, as his top assistant in the Navy Department, Roosevelt appointed Louis Howe. Louis could not tell a bow from a stern, but he knew all about patronage. Deserving relatives of Democratic friends were soon filling the roster at the Brooklyn Navy Yard.

The effort was wasted. Mistakenly imagining that Tammany was on the ropes as a result of Wilson's victory, Roosevelt entered the primary for governor as an anti-Tammany Democrat. He hoped Boss Murphy would put up William Randolph Hearst, king of New York's yellow press, whom he felt sure he could beat. But Murphy crossed him up by picking James W. Gerard, a respectable Tammany stalwart serving as ambassador to Germany. During the campaign Gerard made headlines helping Americans stranded in Europe by the outbreak of war, and from three thousand miles away breezed to victory. The only dividend the Roosevelt-Howe team got was experience.

But the war took away the sting of defeat. Roosevelt was dedicating the anchor of the *Maine* in Reading, Pennsylvania, when the news reached him. Hurrying back to the department, he found "as I expected . . . everything asleep and apparently oblivious to the fact that the most terrible drama in history was about to be enacted." Just what needed to be done in such a hurry was not clear, but according to the youthful assistant secretary neither his boss, nor his boss's friend William Jennings Bryan, Secretary of State, had any concept of what a big European war meant.

What it meant to Roosevelt was an opportunity to expand the Navy. There was still a touch of the *Harvard Crimson* in Roosevelt's gung ho enthusiasm for the Navy; he was distinctly persona grata with Colonel Thompson's Navy League. Those patriotic steel and munitions tycoons thought America should have a navy "second to none," in other words, as big as the enormous, expensive British Navy. They cited the immense historical work composed by retired American naval officer Alfred Thayer Mahan, *The Influence of Sea Power on History*. Franklin Roosevelt, who had received Mahan's

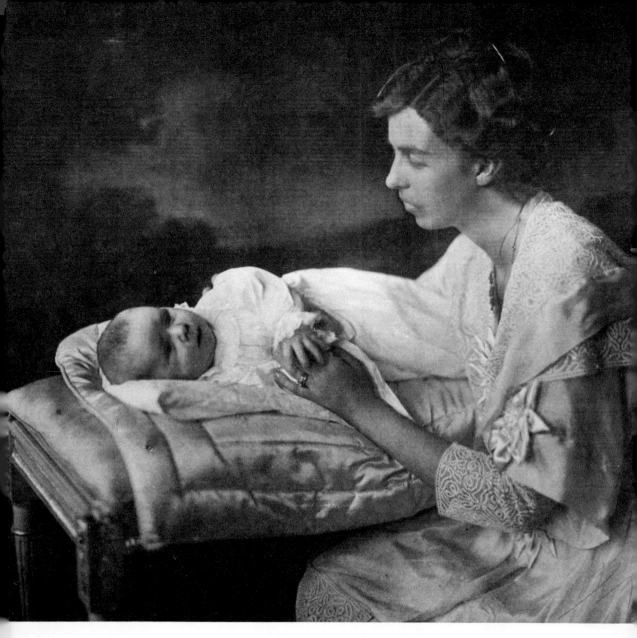

Eleanor and Franklin Roosevelt, Jr., 1914

volumes as a gift at Harvard, had entered into correspondence with the author. For Mahan and the Navy League, a nation's stature was measured by the number of battleships in its fleet, a notion Roosevelt enthusiastically endorsed. He loved battleships. "The big gray fellows were magnificent as they went past, with all hands at the rail, and I only wish a hundred thousand people could have seen them," he rhapsodized after a review.

Three generations of Roosevelts in Washington, 1916. The children, left to right, are Elliott, Franklin, Jr., James, John, and Anna.

Josephus Daniels, who was even less sailorly than Louis Howe, saw nothing lovable about a hulking mass of steel and machinery which cost a fortune and was useful for nothing except to try to sink another such mass. A homely, old-fashioned figure in black slouch hat and string tie, a teetotaler never seen on the Washington cocktail circuit, Daniels was not appreciated by Roosevelt till long after. But Daniels was a genuine liberal Democrat, who braved the outrage of the admirals by taking away the officers' liquor privilege, and their contempt by attacking the problem of VD among the enlisted men. Toward the patriotic bombast of Teddy Roosevelt, Daniels maintained a healthy pacifist skepticism, and toward Teddy's impetuous young relation a tolerant restraint.

F.D.R. with Charles F. Murphy, his old foe, and John A. Voorhis at Tammany Hall, July 4, 1917

F.D.R. and Clark Griffith, manager of the Washington Senators, raise the flag at the opening of the 1917 baseball season.

A moment for relaxation: on the rifle range, 1917

*On an inspection tour of Cuba, Haiti, and Santo Domingo,
January–February 1917*

*Roosevelt greets a welcoming
crowd during an inspection
tour of an ordnance plant
at Bridgeport, Connecticut,
May 20, 1918.*

"My chief [Josephus Daniels] and myself in the act of casting longing glances at the White House."

Lending support to the 1918 Liberty Loan Drive are Douglas Fairbanks and Mary Pickford, (kneeling) Marie Dressler and Charlie Chaplin.

From at least the sinking of the *Lusitania* (a wildly lucky, or unlucky, U-boat feat of May 1915), battle lines were drawn between U.S. hawks and doves. The hawks included Colonel Thompson, T.R., Senator Henry Cabot Lodge, General Leonard Wood, and Colonel Robert R. McCormick, old Grotonian and publisher of the Chicago *Tribune*. The most prominent dove was Secretary of State Bryan, who resigned in protest against the strong *Lusitania* note. Possibly the second most prominent was Daniels. Roosevelt was not slow in aligning himself with the hawks, with whom he lunched and dined, sometimes being so indiscreet as to drop information that Republican congressmen used against the Administration.

By 1916 he was ready, like Uncle Teddy, to "uphold U.S. rights," i.e., declare war. Wilson was not. But the aggressive posture of the young Assistant Secretary of the Navy was of value to the Administration; it made him an ideal spokesman to rebut campaign charges that Wilson was neglecting "preparedness." This marked an advance in his career—he was now an asset to the party on a national scale.

But no sooner was the election over than he was maneuvering behind Daniels' back to get the Navy closer to the war. He sought permission from Wilson to move the fleet from its Cuban base to Atlantic waters, and uncovered a constitutional loophole to permit arming American merchantmen with Navy guns and gun crews.

Early in 1917 the German decision to adopt "unrestricted submarine warfare" virtually ended the Great Debate in the United States. The Germans had some logic on their side—the British were hunting U-boats with fake merchantmen flying the American flag— but the torrent of propaganda in the press wiped out rational discussion. Surrendering to the pressure, Wilson asked Congress for a declaration of war. Six senators and fifty congressmen, led by "Fighting Bob" La Follette of Wisconsin, voted no. La Follette, whose white mane gave him the look of a lion, and who had the courage of one, coolly took up four hours of the Senate's time to refute Wilson's speech point by point. But as the British ambassador and a coterie of Washington socialites in evening dress filed into the gallery, more orthodox senators loosed a torrent of patriotic rhetoric, and the nation went to war.

On N Street the children played soldier and Eleanor knitted socks for doughboys. She was so conscientious about following the government's directives on saving soap and not eating meat that a *New York Times* girl correspondent wrote a gushy story which appeared under a headline: "How To Save In Big Homes"—"Food Administration Adopts Mrs. F. D. Roosevelt's Plan as Model." The text detailed how Eleanor encouraged her ten servants (the *Times* must have counted the Hyde Park and 65th Street establishments too) to be on the lookout for possible savings, to find uses for leftovers, to serve no bacon, to have cornbread on the menu every day, and to cut down on laundry soap. The story appeared after Eleanor's annual departure with the children for Campobello. Roosevelt, who took a lot of kidding, wrote her: "All I can say is . . . I am proud to be the husband of the Originator, Discoverer, and Inventor of the New Household Economy for Millionaires! Please have a photo taken showing the family, the ten cooperating servants, the scraps saved from the table . . . I will have it published in the Sunday Times." Not long before, the grocer had come to the door of 1733 N Street to remind the occupants of an unpaid bill, and Roosevelt had experimented with coming home for lunch to save money. His salary was $5500 a year and their combined *rentier* incomes only about $13,000 (of which the larger part was Eleanor's).

Downtown, Roosevelt plunged into the task of getting the Navy on a war footing with such zeal that Wilson had to intervene to make sure the Army, lacking such a bureaucratic dynamo, got its share of procurement. Besides energy, Roosevelt demonstrated first-rate administrative talent along with imagination and a capacity for thinking big. He pushed for more battleships, more cruisers, and more destroyers, in harness with the admirals, the Navy League, and the British, who were beginning to worry as the U-boats sank record tonnages of unescorted merchant ships. He also pushed for the construction of an enormous fleet of small power boats to patrol U.S. harbors from Portland to Galveston, a project on which Josephus Daniels put a damper. An even bigger, and much better idea (and more original with Roosevelt) was a vast network of mines to keep U-boats out of the Atlantic by blocking the entire North Sea between Scotland and Norway. At first both American and British admirals pronounced the scheme half-baked, but on adequate study it turned out to be entirely practical, except that by the time mine-laying operations were begun the war was over. The U-boat menace had been met by the obvious but tardily adopted convoy system.

Still another Roosevelt brainstorm was both original and effective. By employing Navy cargo ships to take coal to distant bases he could use the same bottoms to bring back tin from Malaya, nitrates from Chile, and other critical raw materials. He had already made an important contribution to true preparedness by setting up a stockpiling system.

But despite the ideas he hatched and the hard work he put in, he was not at all satisfied to be Assistant Secretary of the Navy during a war. Uncle Teddy thrilled the Harvard Club in New York with

Roosevelt disembarks at the Pauillac, France, Naval Air Station, August 14, 1918.

U.S.S. Nevada

Roosevelt inspects a naval railway battery in 1918. The Navy operated on land in World War I, and officers attached to the battery wore Army uniforms.

Roosevelt in Paris, August 1918. Getting near the fighting was the next best thing to donning a uniform.

the announced intention of raising a "Roosevelt Division" of "mounted infantry" (there appearing to be little need for cavalry in the present war, "mounted infantry" seemed the most Roosevelt thing possible). Franklin Roosevelt wanted a commission in the heavy artillery, which was employing naval guns. But Wilson callously turned down Uncle Teddy's offer to be the hero of the war, and Josephus Daniels, who had put up with a good bit from the younger Roosevelt, nevertheless valued him and refused to give him up. The best that restless Franklin could swing was a trip to Europe in the summer of 1918 which, despite some genuine functional aspects in connection with war zone bases, supply, and inter-Allied relations, had many of the earmarks of a junket. From the crossing aboard a zigzagging destroyer through meetings with King George, Marshal Joffre, Clemenceau, and

Lloyd George to a visit to the front where he saw dead bodies and had to take cover from artillery shelling, the expedition was bully; in later years the hazards grew with the telling. One interesting lesson the trip might have had for him he missed. This was an inter-Allied argument over the naval command in the Mediterranean. The British were pressing for a British commander in chief, using as an argument the fact that the Italians were cautiously keeping their fleet in port. The Italians answered that they saw no reason to bring their ships out, in view of the fact that there were no enemy ships in the Mediterranean. The French pointed out that they had the most battleships in the Mediterranean, so why should there be a British naval commander there? Roosevelt helped work out a compromise solution, but he did not get the point of the argument. The trouble was that the British had had to give in, very late and with considerable reluctance, to the necessity of putting their army group on the Western Front under a French commander in chief, Foch, and were looking for a little quid pro quo somewhere. The pettiness and intensity of jealousy in a war fought by allies were well illustrated; they would arise critically in the next World War, with Roosevelt in the decision-making position.

A severe attack of flu suspended his further efforts to get into uniform until October, when President Wilson turned down his formal request on the grounds that peace was imminent.

DURING the war a dramatic episode either took place, or did not take place, in Roosevelt's private life. In *This Is My Story* Eleanor records that soon after she came to Washington she found that "it took me such endless hours to arrange my calling list, and answer and send invitations, that I finally engaged [a secretary] for three mornings a week." That is all Eleanor says, a circumstance which may be cause for suspicion. The secretary was a slim, rosy-cheeked twenty-three-year-old blonde named Lucy Page Mercer. Daughter of an impoverished and broken-up family of the Washington aristocracy, Lucy had grown up in the very 1700 block of N Street where the Roosevelts lived, and enjoyed a status that permitted her to mix socially with her employers and their friends. She went along on yacht parties in Chesapeake Bay in the summer, including occasions when Eleanor was at Campobello with the children. Roosevelt mentioned her presence freely in writing Eleanor ("Lucy Mercer was along, with the Graysons . . ."), a circumstance which may disarm suspicion.

Thirty years later, after Roosevelt's death, a rumor began to spread. Roosevelt, it was said, fell in love with Lucy and wanted to marry

43

An early photograph of Lucy Mercer Rutherfurd

her, but either Eleanor refused to give him a divorce or Lucy, a Catholic, could not marry him, or both. Frank Freidel, distinguished historian and author of what will undoubtedly be the definitive multivolume biography of Roosevelt, does not believe it. Jonathan Daniels, son of Roosevelt's boss at the Navy Department, member of Roosevelt's staff in the Presidential years and distinguished, if nonacademic, historian himself, does. He quotes a North Carolina cousin of Lucy's, Elizabeth Cotten: "She and Franklin were very much in love . . . I know that a marriage would have taken place, but as Lucy

44

said to us, 'Eleanor was not willing to step aside.' . . . There was never anything secret or clandestine . . . as far as Mrs. Roosevelt was concerned. They were frank and honorable . . . it was real love . . . and . . . it lasted through the years."

There is substantiation at least for the fact that Lucy Mercer, who married and became Lucy Rutherfurd, remained a friend, and evidently a close friend, of Franklin Roosevelt "through the years." Once as President he even stopped his Hyde Park-bound special train in New Jersey to pay her a visit. Lucy was not only pretty, perhaps beautiful, but she had a gift that Eleanor, with all her great qualities, lacked—the enjoyment of fun and laughter. James Roosevelt, alluding to his father's predilection for the company of daughter Anna, assorted daughters-in-law, nieces, and women cousins, coined a nice phrase, "the touch of triviality" that they brought a man under pressure.

If over-serious Eleanor was indeed confronted with a problem in Lucy, she probably handled it with common sense, a gift she definitely did have. Divorce for a father of five would (in 1920) have written finish to a political career. As it is, the most extraordinary feature of the whole story is its tardiness in appearing. Even neutral journalists during the New Deal years would have given an arm for it. Yet the first hint came in a book by a newspaperman's widow in 1946. Whatever happened, if anything did, was certainly cloaked by a truly Victorian discretion.

4

The Making of a Future President

AMID the usual disorder of a Democratic national convention,
Delegate Franklin Roosevelt was wandering around the floor
when he encountered Judge Ansberry, a lieutenant of Governor
Cox of Ohio, who had just been nominated for President. Peremptorily the judge demanded: "How old are you?"

"Thirty-eight," said Roosevelt. "Why?"

"I'm going to nominate you for vice-president."

As Roosevelt hastily made his way out of the hall in obedience to
convention etiquette (the 1920 scene was San Francisco), Ansberry
made his nominating speech. Cox had taken the precaution of
checking out his choice of running mate with Boss Murphy.
Only a few days earlier Roosevelt had offended the old boss by wres-
tling the New York standard from a Tammany fist and parading it in
a floor demonstration for President Wilson. Murphy told Cox's
emissary: "I don't like him, but this is the first time a Democratic
nominee for the Presidency has shown me courtesy. I would vote
for the devil himself if Cox wanted me to."

Colonel McCormick's Chicago *Tribune* waxed sarcastic over the
Democrats' pre-empting the Roosevelt name: "He is [there] to put
the honey of a name on the trap of a ticket. . . . If he is Theodore
Roosevelt . . . Bryan is a brewer." There was some truth in that,
but the new Roosevelt had added some luster of his own to the name.
He was widely and reasonably credited with the fact that the United
States had emerged from the war with that "second to none" fleet
that the Navy League had advocated (including a large number of
destroyers destined to play a tremendous role twenty years later),

46

and he had given strong backing to the Navy's history-making NC-4 flight, the first transatlantic air crossing, the previous year (1919). Another angle to Cox's choice was the inevitable geographic factor. The Republicans had also nominated an Ohioan, silver-haired Senator Warren Harding, and balanced him with tight-lipped Cal Coolidge of Massachusetts.

The issue in the campaign was supposed to be the League of Nations, in whose passionate defense President Wilson had suffered a thrombosis. Paying a visit to the White House, Cox and Roosevelt presented themselves to the stricken President, slumped in the sunshine under the portico, a shawl covering his paralyzed arm. Cox told him: "Mr. President, we are going to be a million per cent with you, and your Administration, and that means the League of Nations." The gray face came to life for a moment. "I am very grateful," he murmured.

The League was hardly a profitable issue for the Democrats. It was hated by the Irish because it was run by England, by the Germans because it was run by France, and by the Italians because it said Fiume should belong to Yugoslavia. It had enough support, especially in the Midwest and West, so that Harding found it prudent to say nothing either for or against it, but the campaign did not hang on it. What it hung on was high prices, shortages, and all the irritants of the end of a war, aptly summarized by Harding as a desire for a "return to normalcy." Roosevelt campaigned with his usual inexhaustible enthusiasm, covering forty-two states in three months. "I spent eighty-nine out of ninety-two nights in a sleeping car," he recalled. Everywhere people pumped his hand and took him for T.R.'s son, to the immense irritation of T.R., Jr., who had his own political ambitions. Louis Howe refined their campaigning technique by hiring an advance man, a young newspaperman named Steve Early, who wired back advice on the speeches ("New Hampshire is hopeless. The Irish are rampant . . .").

The most intriguing incident of the campaign took place in Butte, Montana. Answering a familiar complaint that Great Britain enjoyed six votes in the League (India, Australia, etc.), Roosevelt was reported as tossing off an observation that the Latin-American countries would vote the way the United States wanted them to, and that his own Navy Department controlled a couple of Latin votes. He was even quoted as bragging that he had written Haiti's constitution. He promptly repudiated the AP dispatch, and the affair had no impact on a hopeless campaign, but it pointed up some interesting changes going on in the world and in Roosevelt.

The Haitian constitution, which had indeed been written in Wash-

On the dock at Campobello

ington, and which Roosevelt had approved, had reduced the tiny country to a U.S. protectorate, occupied by the Marines. Roosevelt had junketed there to award a medal to General Smedley Butler for surprising and massacring two hundred Haitians, and congratulated Butler on building a road under forced-labor conditions which Butler himself said it "would not do to ask too many questions" about. But now, in the aftermath of the war for which liberals were trying to find some ex post facto justification, the imperialist style of T.R. ("I took Panama") seemed out of date. Whether or not Roosevelt really said the words attributed to him that night in Butte, he knew better.

So sweeping was the "return to normalcy" flood that Harding captured over two thirds of the entire vote outside the South, including, to Roosevelt's embarrassment, New York. Looking over the returns at Hyde Park, he concluded that only a depression could give the Democrats another chance nationally. (That sounds more prescient than it was; he was thinking of the small-scale depressions

48

F.D.R. gets a helping hand.

Sailing at Campobello.

of the past, one of which the Republicans survived, in 1921–22, without much pain.)

Back once more in New York and Hyde Park after eight years in Washington, he seized the opportunity for family togetherness; he taught the boys hockey on the pond, and tobogganed down the long slope to the Hudson (everybody aboard except Eleanor) with Roosevelt abandon. On the steep run back uphill he set so fast a pace the boys' lungs ached with the cold air. Spills were treated as part of the fun.

He was no great disciplinarian, but he inspired respect along with affection. Once James stole ten dollars from his father's wallet to buy Anna something she especially wanted for Christmas. Dad called the boy into the study, asked him where he got the money, and

At Waldbreitbach, Germany,
January 1919 to
supervise naval demobilization

With President and Mrs. Wilson,
returning from Europe on the
U.S.S. George Washington,
February 1919

F.D.R. joins President Wilson in reviewing a Marine brigade of
Chateau Thierry veterans. Washington, August 12, 1919.

At a review in Washington for the visiting Prince of Wales (center).
F.D.R. is on the left. November 1919.

waited. James found he couldn't lie. He took a stern lecture, paid
back the money from his allowance, never pilfered again, and Dad
never told anybody.

Roosevelt had no difficulty finding a job. A Democratic business
tycoon named Van Lear Black hired him as vice-president in charge
of the New York office of his Fidelity & Deposit Company, at the
handsome salary of $25,000 a year. In July, Roosevelt returned
to Washington to defend his Navy Department record against Republican charges of a liquor-drug-homosexuality scandal in wartime
Newport, Rhode Island. ("Details are Unprintable," prissily observed
The New York Times.) The Republicans published their report
damning the Navy Department without waiting to hear Roosevelt's
testimony, sending him back to New York considerably irritated. After two weeks in the office, he sailed in Van Lear Black's yacht to
Campobello, where Eleanor and the children were waiting. When the
skipper had trouble finding his way in a fog, Roosevelt took the helm
and brought the craft safely through the Bay of Fundy into harbor.

51

The Roosevelts in Washington, 1919

Next day family and guests went fishing for cod. Roosevelt baited hooks for the guests, who were divided between fore and aft cockpits of the motor launch. To cross back and forth he had to squeeze past the hot engine on a narrow plank. Suddenly he slipped and went into the bay. He pulled himself back aboard at once, his head not even going under, but the icy water shocked his overheated body. "It seemed paralyzing," he recalled years later.

That was Tuesday, August 9, 1921.

The guests departed next morning, and the Roosevelt family went sailing in their little sloop *Vireo*. Heading home they spotted a forest fire on one of the small islands and, as Eleanor recorded, "of course we had to make for shore at once and go fight the fire. We reached home around four o'clock and my husband, who had been complaining of feeling logy and tired for several days, decided it would do him good to go in for a dip in the land-locked lake called Lake Glen Severn, inside the beach on the other side of the island. The children were delighted and they started away. After their swim Franklin took a dip in the Bay of Fundy and ran home."

The idea of curing fatigue by jogging two miles across country, going swimming twice, and jogging home may seem a little weird in the latter part of the twentieth century, but in 1921 the prescription would have been widely approved, and viewed as especially appropriate to a Roosevelt. True, Uncle Teddy had suddenly died a year and a half earlier at the age of sixty, but his simple-minded cult of chest-beating physical exercise lived on.

This time it proved a failure. "I didn't feel the usual reaction, the glow I'd expected," Franklin Roosevelt recalled later. "When I reached the house the mail was in, with several newspapers I hadn't seen. I sat reading for a while, too tired even to dress. I'd never felt quite that way before."

"In a little while," Eleanor wrote, "he began to complain that he felt a chill and decided he would not eat supper with us but would go to bed and get thoroughly warm. He wanted to avoid catching cold. . . .

"The next day my husband felt less well. He had quite a temperature and I sent for our faithful friend, Dr. Bennett, in Lubec." Dr. Bennett diagnosed a cold. Eleanor, not much reassured, sent the children camping so she could nurse the invalid.

The day after that, Friday, August 12, he could not stand up. His legs were painfully sensitive to touch, yet he could not move them. Hearing that a prominent Philadelphia physician was staying at nearby Bar Harbor, Eleanor solicited his help. He diagnosed a blood clot in the lower spinal cord and prescribed massage.

By this time Louis Howe had hastened over from his own place at Horseneck Beach. Eleanor and Louis took turns massaging the stricken man's feet and legs, an extremely painful procedure, and what was worse, a ghastly mistake. The massaging permanently damaged muscle tissue that might otherwise have recovered.

Louis Howe had the wit to look further for medical help. He wrote graphically descriptive letters to Frederic Delano, Roosevelt's uncle, which Delano showed to New York specialists. The specialists at once suspected polio, or infantile paralysis as it was then called. The massages were mercifully canceled. On August 25, fully two weeks after the onset of the illness, a Boston specialist confirmed the diagnosis.

The seriousness of the situation was even then masked by the

The summer of 1920 offered a brief respite at Campobello before a hectic fall of campaigning.

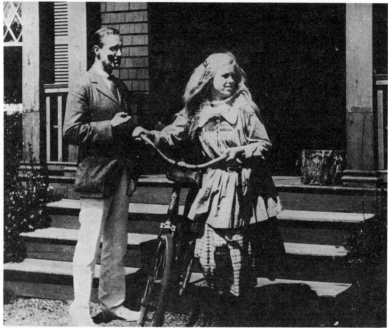

F.D.R. was formally notified of his nomination for Vice-President at Hyde Park on August 9, 1920.

Sara Roosevelt, the family, and Chief at Hyde Park, 1920

One of the more than 800 speeches F.D.R. made during the 1920 campaign

F.D.R. relaxes with Louis Howe, Thomas Lynch, and Marvin McIntyre while on the campaign trail.

difficulty of assessing polio in its early stages. The Boston specialist's prognosis was a mild case, with excellent chances for complete recovery after an adequate period of rest in bed.

Everyone cheered up. Louis Howe moved in on a permanent basis, and Eleanor found the sardonic, chain-smoking gnome a godsend in the crisis. Between them, they worked out a plan and implemented

The 1920 campaign was an exhilarating time for F.D.R. Election results were disastrous for the Democrats, but Roosevelt became a nationally known figure.

it with remarkable success. News of Roosevelt's condition would be kept from the papers until recovery was under way, and he would otherwise be insulated from outside contacts to guard against deep depression. For anyone, but above all for a man of Roosevelt's physique and temperament, the sudden decay into helplessness and dependence threatened psychological catastrophe. Intercepting Sara Roosevelt at the dock on her return from a European trip, Louis with extraordinary address broke the news and sold her on the invincibly cheerful line that he and Eleanor had adopted, and that Roosevelt had promptly embraced. From Campobello, Sara wrote her brother: "I got here yesterday at 1:30 and at once . . . came up to a brave, smiling, and beautiful son, who said: 'Well, I'm glad you are back, Mummy, and I got up this party for you!' He had shaved himself and seems very bright and *keen*. Below his waist he cannot

*Franklin, Jr., and John receive
certificates as founders of the
Woodrow Wilson Award. Income from
the fund created by public subscription
finances the Woodrow Wilson Fellowships*

move at all. His legs (that I have always been proud of) have to be moved often as they ache when long in one position. He and Eleanor decided at once to be cheerful . . . so I have fallen in and follow their glorious example. . . . Dr. Bennett just came and said, 'This boy is going to get all right.' They went into his room and I hear them all laughing. Eleanor in the lead."

Sara innocently assumed that her stricken son would now retire from both business and politics and take up the placid life of a country squire at Hyde Park. Roosevelt never considered such a retreat. Barely a month after his attack, still fully immobilized, he accepted membership on the Executive Committee of the New York State Democratic party. The next day Louis and Eleanor had him transported to Presbyterian Hospital in New York. Military secrecy shrouded the move. Only the children watched as their father was carried out of the house on a stretcher, and for their benefit he kept

Lt. Gov. George Lunn, F.D.R., Presidential candidate John W. Davis, and Al Smith at Hyde Park a month after the stormy Democratic convention

With Dr. William McDonald (right), who treated F.D.R. during the summers of 1925 and 1926 with exercises he had devised for polio patients

Franklin Roosevelt, 1924

it light—his favorite fedora on his head, his current Scottie cradled in his arms, his cigarette holder at a jaunty angle, chin sticking out, a big good-by smile on his face. By motor launch, railroad baggage car, and private limousine he reached the hospital. Only then did Howe release the news, coupled with an unqualified medical prognosis of complete recovery.

He did, in fact, begin progress, but it was infinitely slower and more painful than the doctors anticipated. At the end of October, when he was moved to the 65th Street house, he was able with help to climb from bed into a wheelchair. Small as the gain was, it was important. Louis Howe's political instinct accurately warned that vital to Roosevelt's future was the picture of a man recuperating from an illness rather than one stricken with an incurable disease. At the same time Roosevelt's moral courage—he later told Frances Perkins that he believed "Divine Providence had intervened to save him from total paralysis, despair and death"—built on the hope of eventual total recovery. His cheerfulness surpassed even that of Louis and Eleanor. Friends, arriving with falsely bright faces, went away with genuinely bright ones.

He was especially careful with the children. He made a game of his affliction, pulling back the covers to show them which muscles of his legs were affected, giving them the anatomical names, pointing out signs of progress. He got down on the floor and Indian-wrestled with the boys. Home from Groton for the holidays, Jimmy tried unsuccessfully to be offhand. His father just stretched out his arms: "Come here, old man!" Jimmy rushed forward, cried a little, and was soon chattering about school.

In January (1922) the patient had to have his legs encased in plaster casts to keep unused, uncontrolled muscles from slowly tightening and doubling up his knees. In February he was fitted with steel braces, from hips to feet, with whose aid he learned to stand erect and to walk with crutches.

Doggedly he clung to the illusion of real recovery. Sara and Eleanor, who by now knew better, maintained a resolute feminine pretense. Eleanor was sure that out of sight, in her house next door, Sara "wept many hours," and even iron-willed Eleanor finally broke down in the midst of reading to the two youngest boys, and sobbed uncontrollably. Bathing her face in cold water she sternly cut off her "emotional jag."

It was a tough winter. As Eleanor switched from hostility to alliance with Louis Howe, Sara's resentment of the two grew. She had never favored a political career for her son anyway, and now she thought it madness. She wanted to get him out of the 65th Street house she had furnished and back to Hyde Park, where he could have the peace and quiet he needed for the life of a wealthy invalid. He could devote himself to his collecting, be wheeled about the grounds, and perhaps be helped through an annual European trip. In her hatred of Louis Howe, Sara was not above inspiring Anna Roosevelt to complain about the intruder having a better room than she did. But Sara fought a losing battle. If Louis Howe was valuable to Franklin Roosevelt before polio, he was indispensable afterward.

61

On the houseboat Larooco *off Florida, F.D.R. admires Elliott's catch.*

U.P.I.

Roosevelt riding over the more than 1000 acres he bought to establish the Georgia Warm Springs Foundation

In the midst of his affliction, Roosevelt pondered continually the affliction of the Democratic party. The Republicans were profiting from boom times, even though the boom excluded large elements of the population. Besides Republican prosperity, the Democrats were as usual suffering from disunity. The two party factions were more clearly distinguished and more mutually hostile than ever. The Western and Southern wing, made up mostly of debt-ridden farmers, was Prohibitionist like the Republicans. The Northeast and Midwest wing, centered in the immigrant-crowded big cities, was vehemently Wet. A religious cleavage closely followed the same lines, the big-city Democrats mostly Catholic, especially Irish and Italian, while the rurals were mostly Protestant and in the South almost solidly "native American." Among these the Ku Klux Klan was experiencing a spectacular revival, aimed partly at keeping the Negroes in their place (several lynchings a year attested to the continuing reign of terror in the South) and partly at combatting the very immigrants, Catholic and Jewish, who formed the other wing of the Democratic party. At the national convention of 1924 in New York, the grotesque record of 103 ballots was achieved as the Ku Klux rurals, backing Wilson's son-in-law McAdoo, grimly hung on against the challenge of Wet Catholic Al Smith, who had vaulted to the fore by a smashing victory in the New York governorship race of 1922. Smith supporters packed the gallery of Madison Square Garden ("You couldn't get in unless you wore a Smith button or your collar backwards," said a bitter McAdoo man). The emotion-charged deadlock ended with the exhausted enemies accepting a conservative Wall Street lawyer from West Virginia, John W. Davis, whose nomination guaranteed another Democratic debacle.

But if the convention of 1924 was fatal to the party, it was a personal triumph for Roosevelt. Boss Murphy having died, Smith needed someone to manage his floor fight, and he picked respectable, sympathy-attracting, Wasp Roosevelt. More, when a scheduled orator also died suddenly, Smith asked Roosevelt to make his nominating speech. Hobbling to the rostrum on his crutches and steel leg braces, Roosevelt won a prolonged ovation before saying a word. His speech was made memorable by the felicitous designation of Smith as the "Happy Warrior for his political battlefield." That, plus his gentlemanly conduct of Smith's floor fight, in which he tirelessly sought to hold down the bitterness, made Roosevelt easily the outstanding figure at the convention. His sincere determination to run for no office until he was fully recovered helped elevate him above the snarling factionalism.

In his quest for recovery he spent a small fortune. A Boston specialist recommended hydrotherapy, and in partnership with a Groton-Harvard classmate he bought a houseboat and cruised Florida waters, exploring deserted beaches where he could swim and crawl around in the sand. He took along Jimmy and Elliott, and sometimes Anna—Eleanor had to stay home with the younger children. His correspondence, unceasingly voluminous, required a secretary, and pretty, bright "Missy" LeHand, a member of the 1920 campaign staff, became a permanent member of the family. The cruises were fun—the crippled, helpless skipper never quit laughing it up—but they didn't seem to do much good therapeutically.

Then he heard about a run-down resort in Georgia called Warm Springs, where water highly charged with minerals spouted at a temperature of 80 degrees Fahrenheit. Roosevelt went there and swam in the pool and was immediately enchanted. "I walk around in water four feet deep without braces or crutches," he wrote home with unconscious pathos. A newspaper story about Roosevelt put Warm Springs on the map. Polio sufferers began coming there and Roosevelt, assisting in solving the problem of how to lodge them, conceived the idea of a foundation-supported treatment center. A convention of orthopedic surgeons in Atlanta gave him a chance to sell Warm Springs to the medical establishment. The project took money, so much as to arouse concern in the family—Sara wondered if the children would be able to go to college. But Roosevelt had fallen doubly in love, first with Warm Springs, and second with helping people. In the mineral pool he taught children and grown-ups to swim; he helped them hold their legs straight and wade through the supporting water. Even while making bitterly small progress himself, he thrilled to the progress of others. Years later, when he visited hospitals filled with wounded veterans of the Second World War, it came naturally to him to reassure them in his confident, booming voice, "You'll make it, brother!"

The psychological effect of polio on Franklin Roosevelt can only be a subject for speculation. At the same time that he was battling polio he was undergoing the normal process of maturing. The impatient thirty-three-year-old who had brashly sought a seat in the U.S. Senate in 1914 had in 1928 been replaced by a grown-up man. Yet polio certainly taught him something. His natural optimism, tempered by pain, quenched by disappointment, emerged stronger than steel. A friend recalled long after how Roosevelt had found himself without any means of getting from the dinner table to the living room. With a joking reference to his legs, he slid from his chair, and supporting himself on his hands used his muscular shoulders to drag his body along the floor, then climbed into a chair in the other room.

Surrounded by friends and neighbors at Warm Springs, November 1928

The friend, finding it difficult to conceal his feelings, hastily pretended he heard a telephone ring somewhere.

Roosevelt had made up his mind not to return to politics in 1928. When Smith became Presidential nominee by default, he pressed Roosevelt to run for governor. Roosevelt refused point blank. Smith would not take "No" for an answer. He deluged Warm Springs with telegrams and phone calls, rallied other Democratic leaders to help persuade Franklin, argued with Louis and Eleanor. The party would nominate capable Herbert Lehman, a New York banker, for lieutenant-governor; Lehman would become acting governor whenever Roosevelt wanted to go to Warm Springs. John J. Raskob, Smith's angel, undertook personally to finance the foundation, relieving Roosevelt of concern. Finally, in desperation, Smith played his

With Basil O'Connor, his law partner, at Warm Springs

trump. He communicated the idea that if Roosevelt turned the party down now, when it needed him, he could not count on the party when he needed it.

Roosevelt gave in. Louis Howe was sure they would lose; nevertheless he threw himself into organizing the campaign with all his normal manic energy. Eleanor, now a seasoned campaigner, helped. So did two professionals, James A. Farley and Edward J. Flynn. Even for a Roosevelt campaign it was strenuous. At the Biltmore headquarters, Howe drove the staff mercilessly; he even had "forgers" whose specialty was signing Roosevelt's name to letters while the candidate was off campaigning upstate.

66

To help him manage the constant in-and-out-of-the-car maneuver, Roosevelt found an invaluable new aide. A tough New York cop named Gus Gennerich was assigned to Roosevelt's motorcycle detail. They made such a hit with each other that Gus quit the police force to join the staff. He addressed his new boss as "pal," which only momentarily took Roosevelt aback; he reciprocated by addressing Gus the same way.

In his speeches Roosevelt extolled Smith's record as governor and denounced the religious issue, which had flared from coast to coast ("Do you want the Pope to come to Washington and move into the White House?" was a typical 1928 political argument). In the election Smith ran well, all things considered—much better than either Davis in 1924 or Cox in 1920. But as Louis Howe had perceptively forecast, he was knifed by the McAdoo Democrats, who sat on their

At Hyde Park, the 1928 Democratic candidate for Governor listens to election returns with his mother and daughter.

hands or joined in the whispers about booze and the Pope. Smith was soundly beaten, with many Southern states spectacularly defecting.

Roosevelt spent election night at the Biltmore. Early in the evening it was apparent that Smith was doomed, and was trailing Hoover even in New York. But Roosevelt was neck and neck with his opponent Albert Ottinger. It seemed impossible that Roosevelt could carry New York while Smith lost the state, and yet at one A.M., as the gang crowded breathlessly around, Ed Flynn drew up a projection that showed this the likely outcome. The upstate returns were tardy. Everyone had the same fear—that upstate Republican officials were holding back to see how many votes they had to produce to overcome Roosevelt's New York City lead. With the scent of victory in the smoky Biltmore air, Roosevelt phoned county sheriffs and wired agents of his Fidelity & Deposit Company to check with county clerks, while Flynn threatened to send "a hundred lawyers" into the dilatory counties. Next morning the final result was still in doubt; not for another two days was it certain that Roosevelt had been elected governor by a razor-thin margin, 25,000 votes out of more than four and a quarter million cast. Ottinger refused to concede for a week.

The psychological effect of the dramatic victory was tremendous. Devoted Democrat Will Rogers sent a contribution for the Warm Springs Foundation, accompanied by a note: "I don't know how the Party can ever get through paying you. . . ."

Louis Howe and Roosevelt had already thought of a way.

5

Roosevelt Takes Command

Although a less than Happy Warrior, Al Smith did not consider himself a dead one. Taking stock in the winter of 1928–29, it seemed to him that he still had a chance at the White House if something unpleasant happened to the Republicans before the next election. In case something did, he took measures to assure himself of a political base. His idea was that Frank, as he called him, was a sweet guy and had a good voice on the *raddio,* but was too crippled to be more than window dressing in Albany. Therefore he proposed that Roosevelt take the oath and pack up for Warm Springs while he himself stayed dutifully on in Albany to coach Lieutenant Governor Herbert Lehman (another sweet guy, but Jewish, so he couldn't run for President either). To keep the party organization securely in his own hands, Al thoughtfully bequeathed his hard-boiled right-hand woman, Belle Moskowitz, as Roosevelt's "secretary."

Al's disillusionment began at once. In defending his choice of Roosevelt the previous summer he had observed that "a governor doesn't have to be an acrobat." He didn't know how right he was. Roosevelt disclosed that his handicap was so slight that he did not even need the help of Belle Moskowitz. Giving back the inaugural address Belle had written for him, he composed his own, and instead of taking off for Warm Springs he stayed on in Albany. He kept most of Smith's old bureaucrats, but allowed no misconceptions about who was running the state government. Further, everybody in the know was soon aware that Louis Howe, living in the 65th Street house in Manhattan, using a downtown office in the

Behind the wheel of his model A Ford at Hyde Park, 1929

State Crime Commission, and making weekly overnight visits to Albany, was the Belle Moskowitz of the new Administration, with everything that implied.

Even more ominous from Al Smith's point of view was the way Roosevelt imposed his personal image on the governorship of New York—"the Empire State," as Al dearly loved to call it. The new governor had Charles Evans Hughes's class without his remoteness, and Al Smith's warmth without his mispronunciations. His affliction, so far from marring the triumphal image, became part of it. Wheeled down the ramp to the waiting limousine in the Executive Mansion driveway, he called out greetings to the reporters, saying what a beautiful evening it was for his drive down the Post Road, along the river to Hyde Park. As Gus Gennerich helped him into the open car, he used his powerful arms and shoulders to swing himself athletically into his seat. Settling his old Stetson on his head, he allowed Gus to arrange the admiral's cloak over his shoulders and, motorcycles roaring away in front, off he went, waving a last good-by with the cigarette holder.

He was determined to make a good record as governor. Much of the legislation he sponsored and maneuvered through the Republican assembly and senate was aimed at helping the state's large farm population. The program fitted snugly into his national ambitions, because the farm problem was the only serious economic problem in the country.

That at least was how it looked from Albany (and Washington) in the spring of 1929. America, it was evident, was the only real

The Governor, Eleanor, and their youngest son, John, in Albany about 1930

F.D.R. was made a chieftain of the Indian tribes of the New York State Reservation during his visit to the State Fair. Undated.

winner in the war, acquiring a vastly expanded industrial plant which was now turning out a bountiful stream of consumer goods—glass-windowed automobiles, radio receivers, disc phonographs, electric toasters, mechanical washing machines, outboard gasoline engines, snapshot cameras, iceless refrigerators, short-skirted dresses, golf clubs, and dollar watches. Factories hummed, salesmen smiled. American cities spread into the countryside in invincibly neat grid-irons of paved streets lined with stucco houses with coal furnaces in their cellars, electric-light switches on their walls, and flush toilets in their bathrooms. The ancient problems of poverty and insecurity seemed on the way to satisfying solution.

Then came the crash. Spectacular though the panic on Wall Street was, the headlines seemed to most of the country more intriguing than alarming. The leaders of opinion explained what was going on: too much speculation had driven stock prices up above what the stocks were really worth, and now they had come down to more realistic levels. It was a healthy readjustment. There was no call for concern. So said President Hoover, and so said an even more impressive

71

With the Roosevelts is his devoted personal secretary,
Marguerite "Missy" LeHand.

authority, Andrew Mellon, the Pittsburgh billionaire who had served as Secretary of the Treasury through nine glorious years of Republican prosperity. The omniscient, anonymous sources of wisdom on the nation's editorial pages echoed Hoover and Mellon.

Presently, however, it began to appear that something was amiss. Christmas business was off, automobile sales down, construction starts canceled. Breadlines and soup kitchens began to appear. Mellon stoutly maintained that the rising unemployment was no more than the seasonal norm; in the spring everything would be all right. Spring came. Unemployment, instead of coming down, went up.

Roosevelt had no more perception of the growing depression than did Hoover and Mellon, possibly less. He liked to think of himself as a man of business experience, on the basis of a few ventures during his period of political idleness. What they had amounted to was speculation, differing from the Wall Street variety more or less in the way horseracing differs from poker. Roosevelt's flyers were of the old-fashioned nineteenth-century "scheme" type—oil wildcatting, German marks, vending machines, advertising space in taxicabs. Most spectacular was an attempt to corner the lobster market, an inspiration that had cost him $25,000. Despite these past ventures he did not hesitate to preach a pious sermon to a church audience in Poughkeepsie on the immorality of stock speculators who tried to get something for nothing.

Fishing at Warm Springs

But as 1930 stretched, spread, and deepened the Depression (the word began to enter the language, and with a capital *D*), Roosevelt awoke to at least one aspect of it. It was making the Republicans unpopular. As the off-year election campaign developed, it became apparent that the Democrats, rather than the Republicans, had the upper hand in New York State. Roosevelt pitted his record as governor, which he fortified with a smooth campaign—the Howe-Farley-Flynn team was now a mature working organization—against a lackluster Republican opponent. But on election eve he stopped Farley from issuing a prediction of victory by 600,000, and was as surprised as anyone when the returns rolled up a Democratic plurality of 725,000.

Farley met the newsmen in the Biltmore with a bold statement, prepared without Roosevelt's knowledge: "I do not see how Mr. Roosevelt can escape becoming the next presidential nominee of his party." Reporters besieged Roosevelt in Albany, and got a deprecating chuckle—it was much too early to talk about such a thing, said the governor. Behind that bland put-on a new outfit began operating in a suite of offices at 331 Madison Avenue. The title on the door was FRIENDS OF ROOSEVELT and the director was Louis Howe. The group had two functions: first, public relations and fund-raising, and second, delegate-hunting. Howe took personal charge of the PR, subletting the delegate-hunting to Farley. A national leader in the Elks, Farley turned a trip to the lodge's convention in Seattle into a reconnaissance of Roosevelt sentiment among the professional politicians.

The 1930 campaign for re-election as governor of New York. On election night a jubilant Roosevelt received word of his victory at the Hotel Biltmore in New York City.

Former Governor and Mrs. Alfred E. Smith, seated at left, were among the honored guests at the inaugural ball in Albany, December 31, 1930. Also seated with the Roosevelts is Franklin's mother, Sara.

He proved to be the perfect man for the job, completely disarming the Westerners who had their preconception of a raucous, hard-drinking, cigar-chewing Tammany boss. Mixing Irish sociability with country-boy friendliness—his background was Rockland County, not Manhattan—Farley neither drank nor smoked, and never forgot a name or a face.

At the same time as Farley's cross-country tour, Howe pulled off a major coup. *Liberty* magazine brought up the health issue; Louis had a star *Liberty* staff writer visit Roosevelt in Albany, and supplied him with a batch of glowing new medical reports. Howe distributed 50,000 copies of the resulting piece, which Farley characterized as "a corker." On top of that Howe got the *Liberty* writer to collaborate with him on a series of articles on national issues under Roosevelt's by-line. Another Louis Howe gimmick was destined for enduring fame. Casting about for a way to exploit his tiger's chief weapon, audio appeal, he hit on the "Fireside Chat"—a friendly, neighbor-to-neighbor report on state affairs delivered from the Executive Mansion or Hyde Park.

By late 1931 Howe and Farley had worked their spring groundswell for Roosevelt into bandwagon proportions. The New York election

WIDE WORLD

*With Tammany leader
John F. Curry at the New York
Young Democratic Club Dinner
at the Hotel Astor,
April 30, 1931*

*The George Washington Bridge was opened October 24, 1931,
by Governor Morgan F. Larson of New Jersey and Roosevelt.*

victories, plus the Roosevelt name and personality, plus plenty of hard work, had made him a front runner. Now the trick was to avoid the disasters that so often tripped front runners.

There were four principal shoals. The first was the League of Nations. Roosevelt was on record as favoring U.S. entry since the 1920 campaign, but the League had grown more and more unpopular in America. The war debts were largely responsible. In 1931

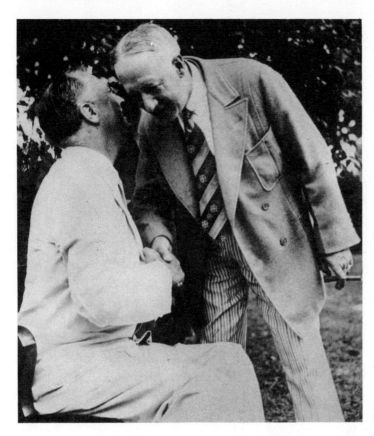

*Al Smith and F.D.R.
greet each other warmly
at a Hampton Bays
luncheon in 1931.*

Hoover reluctantly agreed to a moratorium, suspending payments of inter-Allied debts and German reparations, to save Germany from bankruptcy. A popular radio joke went: "Where is the capital of the United States?" Answer: "All over Europe." The powerful nationalist publisher William Randolph Hearst, a stalwart of the Democratic party, was campaigning against the League as if it were a foreign conspiracy aimed at the United States.

Second was the "wet" issue, which had helped wreck Al Smith. The party's right wing, led by John J. Raskob, Du Pont partner and outgoing national chairman, was determined to write Prohibition repeal into the platform, while most of the Southerners, though by no means averse to a drink, were politically committed to keeping Prohibition.

Third, there was Jimmy Walker. Re-elected mayor of New York by a resounding majority just after the crash, this debonair, glib, but not very smart little showman had brought back corruption on the old-fashioned scale to Tammany Hall. Jimmy night-clubbed in the "speaks," traveled in Europe, hobnobbed with the wealthy with no visible explanation of where the money came from. His Irish followers, delighted to see one of their own in an exalted position,

F.D.R. and his family on the terrace at Hyde Park (1931). Standing, from left, are John, Betsy Cushing Roosevelt, James, Eleanor, Elliott, Curtis Dall, F.D.R., Jr. Seated are Sara, F.D.R. holding "Sisty" Dall, and Anna holding "Buzzy" Dall.

Elliott Roosevelt and Elizabeth B. Donner were married in Villanova, Pennsylvania, January 15, 1932.

cared not at all. "Look at that lad, right up there with the counts and countesses!" a Manhattan bus driver commented admiringly of a tabloid picture of Walker on the Riviera. But Irishness was no excuse to the Protestant Republican Establishment—if anything, the contrary. Under pressure to do something about Walker and his friends, Roosevelt was given a temporary reprieve when the Republican legislature launched an investigation, headed by an anti-Tammany Democrat named Samuel Seabury. Roosevelt could wait till the evidence was collected. But after that he would be hung up between sacrificing respectable support by lenience to Walker, and enraging all the Irish bosses in the country by getting tough.

Fourth, there was the Depression. Liberals in Congress, led by young Bob La Follette and New York's Wagner, were demanding that after two solid years of catastrophic unemployment, the federal government take some steps to relieve misery. But if the federal government spent money to relieve misery, President Hoover pointed out, it would throw the budget out of balance. In his reverence for the federal budget Hoover was not alone. Everybody *knew* the budget had to be balanced. Businessmen and householders who had never balanced their own budgets knew it. The most daring American economist of the day, Professor Paul Douglas of the University of Chicago, went only so far as to think that the government could go into debt during a depression and pay the debt off "rapidly" in prosperous times. Yet, with unemployment at nearly 25%, and the states going broke paying for welfare, there was hardly any alternative to using the federal government's borrowing power.

Any of these four traps could catch an unwary front runner, opening the way to rivals. These had been slow to appear, but they were there. Ohio had no fewer than three favorite sons, the foremost being Newton D. Baker, Wilson's Secretary of War. Texas was extolling John Nance Garner, the squinty, white-eyebrowed new Democratic Speaker of the House. A Chicago banker named Melvin Traylor was for some reason regarded as Presidential timber. Ex-Governor Byrd of Virginia viewed himself as a promising candidate. But by far the most important of Roosevelt's rivals was Al Smith. Roosevelt took care to preserve the "Frank" and "Al" relationship in correspondence, but Al had long since concluded that Frank was a snake he had inadvertently clasped to his shirtfront. And though deprived of his natural political base by Roosevelt's ambition (call it treachery and Al wouldn't hit you), Smith was still formidably popular among Democrats of the big Northeast cities. That gave him a lot of potential in boss-dominated primaries.

On the very first day of the climactic year 1932, the first trap, the

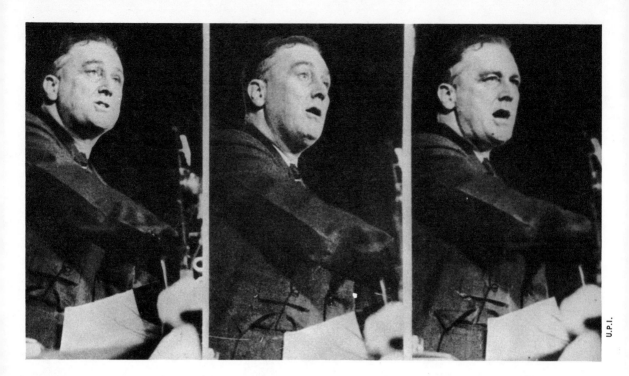

As Judge John E. Mack placed Roosevelt's name in nomination in Chicago, a huge picture of F.D.R. unrolled from the balconies, the organ struck up "Happy Days Are Here Again," and the convention crowd went wild.

F.D.R. became the first Presidential nominee to fly in order to deliver his acceptance speech in person, July 2, 1932.

WIDE WORLD

League of Nations, was sprung. William Randolph Hearst went on the radio to deliver a patriotic diatribe. Amid breadlines, foreclosures, and bankruptcies, the slogan Hearst proposed for the country and its next President was "America First!" Next day a front-page editorial in the 28 Hearst newspapers across the country named Hearst's candidate: John Nance Garner.

Next, Raskob sought to get the national committee to make Prohibition repeal the main thrust of the coming campaign.

Then Judge Seabury turned in his report on Jimmy Walker. The product of more than a year's investigation, and timed to do Roosevelt no good, it was a well-documented, inescapable indictment of a man clearly unfit to be mayor of a large city, or a small one.

Finally La Follette and Wagner, battling valiantly in Congress, got a $750 million unemployment relief bill passed by the Senate, which required borrowing money in excess of anticipated revenues—unbalancing the budget. Though Roosevelt did not have to vote on the measure, not being a congressman, he had to say something. He had to either endorse the thing, and transgress on orthodox economics, or oppose it and alienate the liberals.

One after the other, Roosevelt skillfully evaded all four traps. First, on the League of Nations, he made a straightforward retreat. The League, he announced, had turned away from the noble dream of Woodrow Wilson and taken to bickering over purely European affairs, with which America should have nothing to do. Some of his oldest friends and closest supporters were pained, but not one of his rivals attempted to make capital of his retraction. The League issue, as Roosevelt perceptively saw, was a dead one.

Next he maneuvered successfully against Raskob on Prohibition. Through spies in Raskob's national committee headquarters, he was kept informed of the wealthy chairman's plans. To combat them, Roosevelt made contact with Senator Cordell Hull of Tennessee, already a Roosevelt supporter and an enemy of Raskob on ideological grounds all across the board—Prohibition, the tariff (Raskob incredibly favored the insane Republican Smoot-Hawley high tariff, which had already provoked worldwide retaliation against American goods), and federal unemployment relief. Hull organized the Southern wing of the party; Farley journeyed to Washington to cement the alliance, which he dramatized by sitting next to Hull at the national committee meeting. Raskob and Smith were forced into a strategic withdrawal; Prohibition was eliminated as an issue in the primaries.

The Seabury report on Walker had come in on the very eve of the Democratic convention in Chicago, possibly because Seabury was harboring a personal fantasy about the White House. Roosevelt

Massachusetts boss James M. Curley, Mayor of Boston, confers with F.D.R. in Hampton Beach, New Hampshire, after the convention. July 17, 1932.

cleverly sent the report to Walker to answer, which took care of the convention problem. Walker ostentatiously went to Chicago and voted against Roosevelt, but his bravado soon wilted. In a showdown in Albany, Roosevelt nailed the shifty little New Yorker, who resigned and sneaked off to Europe.

But the most interesting, and significant, of Roosevelt's responses was to the problem of unemployment relief versus budget-balancing. Through all the fencing with Smith, Raskob, and Hearst he was increasingly occupied, both on a practical level as governor of New York, and on a more theoretical level as a man who might a year hence be President, with the vast riddle of the American economy. In a much quoted column Walter Lippmann dismissed Roosevelt's candidacy as that of "a highly impressionable person, without a firm grasp of public affairs . . . a pleasant man who, without any important qualifications for the office, would very much like to be President." The judgment, bad as it looks in the light of history, does not on the face of it seem very brilliant for 1932, yet it was widely nodded over by Democrats as well as Republicans. The key to this view of Roosevelt lies in another phrase in Lippmann's column: "He is not the dangerous enemy of anything." To be an effective President, Walter Lippmann thought, a man had to be a dangerous enemy of somebody or something.

83

*Campaigning in Los Angeles, September 24, 1932 (above),
and getting local support from Poughkeepsie, New York.*

Will Rogers introduces the candidate in Los Angeles' Olympic Stadium during the 1932 campaign. On stage are F.D.R., James Roosevelt, William McAdoo, James Farley, and Rogers.

With an eye to capturing the heartlands, Roosevelt set out by train September 13 for a nationwide speaking tour. At Bellefontaine, Ohio, he meets the press in his private railroad car.

At the Hollywood Bowl, September 24, 1932

U.P.I.

An old-fashioned parade greeted F.D.R. in Indianapolis October 20, 1932, where the largest crowd in the city's history—100,000—listened to his address.

A victim of unemployment sells vegetables in front of a Hoover Club.

Roosevelt sought the miners' vote and made stops throughout West Virginia. Here he greets a miner at Elm Grove.

The notion that a leader in a time of crisis needed guts was widely shared, but it was putting the cart before the horse. Applying a remedy to the novel crisis of the Depression might well require battling the Establishment, but first of all it required finding a remedy. That problem interested almost no one, pundit or politician. It is an outstanding mark of Roosevelt's maturity among the men of that time that he took it seriously. Two months after the Lippmann column, the "Brain Trust" (at first "Brains Trust" but shortened by persistent copy editors) was born.

Its original member was Raymond Moley, a high-domed political science professor whom Sam Rosenman, Roosevelt's young aide-de-camp for Albany affairs, had brought in as a speechwriter (his most remembered contribution was the phrase "Forgotten Man" which he had borrowed from somewhere and stuck in a short talk Roosevelt made on the Lucky Strike radio hour). Moley was not basically an adviser—not being an economist he had no particular advice to give. Howe and Farley, passionately dedicated to political manipulation, were useless for anything more serious. Rosenman and Basil O'Connor, the active partner in Roosevelt's law firm who had also joined the general staff, were bright, able men, but innocent of economics. In short, what was missing from the large and talented Albany crew was somebody who might have some kind of clue to what any 1932 Presidential candidacy had to be about.

Moley mentioned a neighbor on Morningside Heights named Rex Tugwell, who taught in the economics department at Columbia. Roosevelt told him to invite Tugwell to Albany for a weekend.

A few nights later Tugwell accordingly appeared at the dinner table of the Executive Mansion. Eleanor, making her usual bright conversation over her usual culinary disaster, asked Professor Tugwell what he thought of a scheme she and Franklin had been discussing for resettling the unemployed on the land. Each unemployed family, she explained, would be given a plot, a house, and necessary tools. Tugwell did not conceal his skepticism at this amateurish proposal. An evening-long argument ensued. Roosevelt testily asserted that at least the resettled families would have enough to eat, but Tugwell would not grant even that much to people brought up in the city with no farming experience.

A few years earlier Roosevelt might have taken offense at having his pet scheme stepped on. Now he decided Tugwell was just the man he needed. Tugwell was basically an agricultural economist and Roosevelt already had an agriculture expert in the person of Henry Morgenthau, Jr., the son of a Wilsonian diplomat and Democratic party angel. Henry was a fussy, humorless, not terribly bright man

Election Day, 1932.
Franklin and his mother
confidently relax in
the library at Hyde Park.

with a talent for making the interesting sound dull. Tugwell, on the other hand, was a good talker, and Roosevelt, no slight conversationalist himself, was willing to listen.

Through the spring there were long talks, in the evenings sunk in the "Smith plush" of the Executive Mansion salon, in the mornings in Roosevelt's bedroom amid the debris of breakfast, the *Times* and *Herald-Tribune,* and the cigarette stubs (which Tugwell observed Roosevelt extinguishing with the care of a man who could be fatally trapped by a fire). Tugwell expounded his theory of the Depression. His idea was that too much of business's profits had been put into plant expansion and stock-market speculation, and not enough into wages and salaries, leading to a decline in consumption. There were signs of this before the crash. With production exceeding consumption, deflation resulted, just as when consumption exceeded production, inflation was the product. A deflating currency made it progressively more difficult for employers to pay workers, and for farmers to meet mortgages. As laid-off workers and farmers shrank the

89

The President-elect,
*flanked by top strategists
James A. Farley and
Edward Flynn, looks over
the returns.*

*Times Square was jammed on election night as thousands
watched the returns on* The New York Times' *bulletin.*

market further, the circle grew more vicious. In the past, it was true, deflation had run its course in a couple of years, with bankruptcies and foreclosures slowly restoring a balance; surviving banks could once more lend money to surviving businesses and surviving farmers, and the economy could begin to expand once more.

Why the thing went so deep this time was a mystery. Tugwell's belief was that the weight of the accumulated debt was so heavy that it would take much longer than usual to get rid of it by the old-fashioned course of bankruptcy, layoff, and foreclosure. His prescription therefore was "an infusion of buying power." Such an infusion could come from only one source, the federal government, because only the federal government had the borrowing capacity to launch a program on the requisite scale.

Early in the Depression, Roosevelt had accepted the established American dogma that unemployment relief was a "local matter." Three years of trying to cope with New York's terrific relief problem were enough to rid him of that illusion. Now his conviction that the federal government had to use its financial power for relief separated him sharply from Hoover.

As Tugwell summarized it, Roosevelt "did not really have a different view of policy [from Hoover], but he had more human sympathy." He was willing, for the sake of helping people hurt by the Depression, to violate the American moral code of economics. To Wagner he wired his support of the $750 million relief bill. Progressives in and out of Congress applauded.

The business community did not. After three years of Depression, American businessmen had arrived at a formula for meeting the crisis. The government, they said, should "restore confidence." When Roosevelt asked his businessmen visitors such as financier Bernard Baruch how confidence was to be restored, they invariably told him: by reducing government spending, lowering taxes, and balancing the budget. He pointed out that Hoover had been doing just that for three years and things had gotten steadily worse. Baruch said the businessmen were afraid of the Democrats, and in particular of Roosevelt (they apparently did not read Walter Lippmann's column). They feared that, if elected, Roosevelt would commit the sanguine sin —unbalance the budget. Their advice for him was to issue a statement that if elected he would faithfully follow Hoover's policies. Roosevelt thanked them and went to Warm Springs for his annual vacation therapy.

On his return trip he saw another kind of American businessman —farmers whose cotton was selling at six cents a pound, corn at thirty cents a bushel. They turned out in crowds at every whistle stop to take a look at the big man on the observation platform, not the way crowds usually turn out to look at a Presidential contender—a celebrity passing through town—but because they wanted to judge him.

He looked too, at those gaunt, respectable men in faded overalls who didn't mind working fourteen hours a day, but minded losing their farms and not being able to feed their families. He promised to do something for them, and he sounded as if he meant it.

Back in Hyde Park, he told the group something that put his political maneuverings of the spring into a more meaningful light. "I'll be in the White House eight years," he predicted. "When those years are over there'll be a Progressive Party. It may not be Democratic, but it will be Progressive." A political movement that represented a drive for human betterment—that was an ideal to outlast a Depression.

Besides the South—F.D.R. country all the way—Roosevelt had good strength in the Midwest and West. Farley counted up some 660 votes, a clear majority. But the Democrats still operated on their ancient two-thirds rule, which created a situation as full of hidden dangers as a basket of fishhooks. Smith had swept primaries in Massachusetts, Connecticut, and Rhode Island, while Garner, backed by Hearst and McAdoo, had won a tight three-way primary race in California. Added to Texas, California made Garner a contender.

Before Howe and Farley left for Chicago, convention strategy was fixed: Farley would reconnoiter the possibility of abrogating the two-thirds rule, and simultaneously try to peddle the Vice-Presidency. Both moves failed. All the stop-Roosevelt forces, from Smith to McAdoo, joined in such paeans to the sanctity of the two-thirds rule that many people reading the newspapers thought it was part of the Constitution. Chances of a dark-horse nomination leaped, and nobody would talk to Farley about running for Vice-President.

Nevertheless, Howe and Farley sought to press for a decision on the first night. Farley took charge at the front, on the convention floor; Howe remained in the command post high up in the Congress Hotel, looking out on Lake Michigan, with a direct line to Roosevelt in Albany. In the crowded, sweltering room (no air-conditioning in those days) Howe stretched full length on the floor, the phone to his ear, his other ear open to the stream of visitors who came to plead and argue, an ashtray spilling cigarette butts on the carpet next to him. The tension mounted (Sam Rosenman, whose nerve tonic was a chocolate milk shake, drank them "serially") as the oratory on the floor masked feverish wheeling and dealing in the hotel rooms. At intervals Farley returned from the front to pour news into Louis'

*Conferring with Otis Moore
and Ed Doyle, manager
of his farm at Warm Springs*

U.P.I.

*Getting firsthand information on farm conditions
near Atlanta, Georgia, October 24, 1932*

free ear. The first ballot was not begun till nearly dawn. The Roosevelt strength held, but it remained over a hundred votes short of the necessary 770. Two more ballots failed to produce significant changes, and left Farley exhausted by his superhuman efforts to keep slipping delegations in line and to press favorite sons to come over. It was after nine o'clock in the morning when the worn-out mob streamed back to the hotels for catnaps and rumor-mongering.

Tall Jim Farley stretched out on the carpet next to diminutive Louis Howe, seventeen floors above Michigan Avenue, for a desperate, whispered conference. The Smith gang was trying to spread the word that Roosevelt was stopped, that it was only a question of which way the stampede would head. Several Roosevelt delegations were rumored ready to bolt.

93

A rare, quiet time in 1932

Farley argued for another go at Garner on the Vice-Presidency. Howe thought Ritchie of Maryland was a better bet, but finally agreed. Farley sought out Sam Rayburn, Garner's Texas floor leader, and received a surprisingly promising response: "We'll see what can be done."

What had happened was that Roosevelt's series of spring maneuvers was paying off behind the scenes. From his grotesque castle in San Simeon, California, William Randolph Hearst telephoned Garner in Washington that they must back Roosevelt to stave off Smith, who had wrecked Hearst's political career in New York, or Newton Baker, who still believed in the unpatriotic League of Nations. Garner called Rayburn. The Vice-Presidency, he drawled, "isn't worth a quart of warm piss" (F.D.R. roared when he heard that one), but he would take it to prevent a deadlocked convention which might jeopardize Democratic victory in November.

As the balloting opened that night neither the delegates nor the Smith-packed gallery knew anything had happened till California's turn came. William Gibbs McAdoo, California's chairman and Al Smith's mortal enemy since the deadlock in Madison Square Garden, rose and made his way to the platform. Amid a crescendo of boos from the gallery, he announced that California was changing its vote from Garner to Roosevelt. The knife was in Smith's back; bosses and favorite sons hastened to board the bandwagon. Bitterly, Smith refused to make the count unanimous, holding his 190¼ votes to the end. The unhappy warrior returned to New York, where he later joined listlessly in the campaign, perhaps in the hope of becoming Secretary of State. Politically he was wiped out.

The convention atmosphere, clouded by the two-thirds battle and Al Smith's frustration, was cleared by a thunderbolt. Roosevelt flew into Chicago in a tri-motored airplane to deliver his acceptance speech in person. Louis Howe met him at the airport. Louis had discovered that the speech drafted by Roosevelt, Moley, and Tugwell (those amateurs) contained no mention of Woodrow Wilson, the party saint, or the platform which, never mind how inconsistent, was the party's oath of fidelity. Louis had written his own version of the speech; in the limousine to the convention hall they argued fiercely, Roosevelt carrying on his end of the debate between waves to the crowd, and at one point stage-whispering out of the corner of his mouth, "Damn it, Louis, *I'm* the candidate!" Little Louis, who frequently accused his boss of stubbornness (he was once overheard yelling, "Can't you get anything into that thick Dutch skull of yours?"), was twice as stubborn. But as the limousine reached the hall, Roosevelt, leafing hastily through Howe's draft, found that both the key points were on the first page. He took Howe's first page and stuck it on top of the Albany draft. Onstage, he read through the salute to Wilson and the platform ("that admirable document," as Louis had the nerve to call it), then switched smoothly to the Moley-Tugwell-Roosevelt rhetoric.

To the strains of "Happy Days Are Here Again," an inspired choice of campaign song dictated by pure accident, the Democrats hailed their new leader. They felt sure they could win. The Republicans were stuck with Hoover, who was stuck with the Depression. The shantytowns where dispossessed families camped were named "Hoovervilles." Salesmen for Hoover vacuums had doors slammed in their faces.

Finally whatever chance Hoover might have had he threw away with a catastrophic blunder. An enterprising World War I veteran in Portland, Oregon, had conceived the idea of a veterans' march to ask Congress to cash immediately the bonus certificates which, by an absurd arrangement, were not scheduled to mature until 1945. Some eleven thousand veterans made their way to Washington, mostly by riding freight cars. An intelligent Washington chief of police helped them camp on the Anacostia flats and in empty federal buildings

95

U.P.I.

A visit with Max Schmeling, the world heavyweight champion, then training for his fight with Jack Sharkey.

WIDE WORLD

With New York's Lt. Gov. Herbert Lehman and Ethel Merman

while a bill to pay the bonus was passed by the House and killed by the Senate. Most of the veterans straggled homeward, but a hard core, led by a Detroit agitator, stayed on and demonstrated outside the White House. Excitable Secretary of War Hurley urged Hoover

Democratic standard bearers Roosevelt and Garner in Peekskill, New York

to use the Army to clear the men out. Hurley was seconded by General Douglas MacArthur, chief of staff. Undertaking the job in person, MacArthur executed it with an appalling combination of coldblooded efficiency and personal showiness.

Next morning at Albany, Roosevelt shouted from his bedroom for everyone to come see the newspaper pictures. They looked, as he said, "like scenes from a nightmare," with soldiers stamping through smoking debris, hauling off resisters weeping from tear gas, while disheveled, weary women and children stood helpless in the wreckage of their pitiful "homes." The victorious general, immaculately tailored, smiled for the photographers.

The Brain Trust had a meeting scheduled to discuss plans for attacking Hoover in the campaign. Roosevelt said it was no longer necessary. He had once admired Hoover, but now he saw him

97

as "a timid Boy Scout leader" for whom he would feel sorry, if he didn't feel sorrier for those people camping along the roads out of Washington. "They must be sleeping cold," he mused. "It's a wonder there isn't more resentment, more radicalism, in this country, when people are treated like that."

The election was almost an anti-climax. Roosevelt campaigned with vigor, and even abandon—he promised both public works and a cut in government spending. Hoover plaintively squeaked that he had paid all the government's bills on time.

On election night nobody had to stay up very late. By nine o'clock the son Sara Roosevelt had entreated to retire to stamp-collecting had been elected President by a landslide, carrying every state west and south of Pennsylvania.

R OOSEV...
his acceptance spee...
tention. The cliché was so much in...
earlier the same day by somebody nominating...
President. But its very popularity was significant. It cut through
journalistic sophistries and expressed the surging demand of a
hundred million people in trouble that somebody do something,
now. In the Hoovervilles that clung dingily to the big cities, families
tried to keep warm while they slowly starved. Salespeople rearranged
stock sixty hours a week, and took six dollars home on Saturday
night. Grocers helplessly extended credit, tucking slips of paper away
in cigar boxes, and got locked in their refrigerators by amateur
robbers.

One reason for the passivity of the American people that Roosevelt
had observed in connection with the Bonus March was lack of
organization in the cities. What violence there was came in rural
areas like Minnesota and Iowa, where organized farmers struck,
demonstrated, and fought deputy sheriffs over foreclosures. Had
industrial labor been organized there might have been major riots
in Detroit, Pittsburgh, Chicago, and New York.

That there were not was probably lucky. Instead of stimulating
rational action against the Depression, outbreaks might have brought
American fascism, conceivably in the shape of a Democratic Mac-
Arthur-for-President ticket.

The election of Roosevelt did not automatically end the threat.
It gained time. Beneath the outward docility of the winter of 1932–

99

to the
...er 1932.

33, dangerous fury seethed. The most popular target was Wall Street, which nobody had liked much even when it was winning, and which had lost all its prestige by panicking. Now two imperial financial structures cascaded noisily into ruin—that of Insull, based in Chicago, and that of Kreuger, based in Sweden (Wall Street has an extended geography)—rendering worthless hundreds of thousands of shares of stock in thousands of middle-class desk drawers. A succession of other financiers—Harrimans, Wigginses, even Morgan himself—were singed by a Senate investigation which disclosed that multimillionaire bankers and brokers habitually cheated their customers and never paid their income tax.

Angrily, bitterly, hopefully, everybody waited for "that guy Roosevelt." In the interim, a bizarre tragedy emphasized the messianic mission of the newly elected President.

Forced by an archaic constitutional provision to stay in the wings four months after his election, Roosevelt was riding in a parade in Miami when Giuseppe Zangara, a sad kook who had spent years looking for someone to shoot (he had tried for King Victor Emmanuel, Cal Coolidge, and Hoover) at last found a target within range. He missed it. While several other people were hit, including Mayor Cermak of Chicago who died two days later, Roosevelt was

100

unscathed. It seemed an act of Providence. Older newspapermen recalled that he had been near-missed once before—during the Red scare of 1919 he and Eleanor had escaped a bomb meant for Attorney General A. Mitchell Palmer, who lived across the street (and who survived to write the platform Roosevelt ran on in '32).

Then the banks started closing. Banks had been going sour for years—Chicago Presidential hopeful Melvin Traylor had been embarrassingly summoned from the convention to save his Loop bank —but in February of '33 the governor of Michigan startled the country by declaring a statewide bank closing until further notice. Detroit's banks weren't alone. The governors of thirty-seven states rapidly followed the example of Michigan. New York and Illinois, the financial centers, shut their banks down at daybreak of Inauguration Day, Saturday, March 4. Five thousand banks were closed; the others were all wondering what would happen Monday. The New York Stock Exchange opened only long enough for its president, Richard Whitney, to announce that it was closing. The Chicago Board of Trade buttoned up for the first time since 1848.

The stage was set for a saviour, and on to it strode (figuratively) a smiling, confident hero. The day before Inauguration the Roosevelts called on the Hoovers. Relations had cooled considerably since the Sunday night suppers on N Street. At a White House governors' reception in 1932 Hoover had delayed his entrance a half hour trying to force Roosevelt to expose his physical weakness by asking for a chair. Eleanor never forgave Hoover that one. Now Hoover unexpectedly brought in Ogden Mills to discuss the bank problem. Roosevelt turned him off, saying that this was a purely social call and to talk business he would want his own advisers present. Tea was concluded with minimum conversation. Roosevelt, who had brought his son Jimmy along to help him, told Hoover that it took him a little while to get up, and please not to wait. Hoover rose, didn't smile, said, "Mr. Roosevelt, after you have been President for a while, you will learn that the President of the United States waits for no one"—and walked out. "Jimmy wanted to punch him in the nose," Roosevelt told Grace Tully afterwards.

On the ride to the Capitol next day, Hoover froze up on his side of the limousine. He hated the whole day, including the crowd's cheers (there was no problem figuring out whom they were cheering).

Because electronics, which transmitted sound with good fidelity, had not yet mastered video, the new President's voice was of critical importance. Roosevelt's was perfect for the occasion—deep, resonant, with excellent diction, and the touch of class in that Groton *a.*

When Franklin Roosevelt became President in the depths
of the Depression, sights like these were common.

A breadline at Sixth Avenue
and 42nd Street, New York City,
February 1932

Hooverville, New York City

Millions long remembered his "I solemnly swear . . ." with Chief Justice Hughes (who had barely missed being President himself once). Roosevelt came on strong in the Inaugural address. In words written not by Moley but by himself, he paraphrased Thoreau: "The only thing we have to fear is fear itself. . . ." The ring of sincerity made the phrase an inspiration. He gave Wall Street a good kick in the pants: "Rulers of the exchange of mankind's goods have failed through their own stubbornness and their own incompetence, have admitted their failure, and have abdicated. . . . The money changers have fled from their high seats in the temple of our civilization. We may now restore that temple to the ancient truths." What that meant was not too clear, but it sounded good. Hoover had never even managed to sound good.

On specifics, Roosevelt laid out three main ideas—public works for the unemployed, something to raise farm prices, and "strict supervision" of the bankers. Above all, he promised action, and went so far as to warn Congress that if it didn't co-operate, he would demand wartime emergency powers.

That was what the country wanted—action. More than anything else, Roosevelt was determined to meet that want. As soon as the last band had marched by, the last governor had proposed his toast in non-alcoholic inaugural punch, and the last congressman's wife had gushed her good-bys, Roosevelt seated himself at Hoover's desk in the office wing, while Howe, Rosenman, Tugwell, Moley, and the gang settled into the rooms around him. They worked late, but not as late as the people in the Treasury Building, where lights burned all night.

Next day, Sunday, Roosevelt was ready with two headline-making moves. He summoned a special session of Congress and announced a "bank holiday" for the whole United States.

The phrase turned the panic into a picnic. At last the country felt it had leadership, and exciting leadership at that. Congressmen had scarcely taken their seats when the President's message containing the new bank bill arrived. Nobody read it. It was passed by a voice vote in the House, and by a nearly unanimous vote in the Senate. Breaking all legislative records it reached the President's desk for signature in seven hours.

The cautious Federal Reserve was busy printing scrip to take the place of hoarded money. But Roosevelt had a much better solution: He went on the air with a Fireside Chat. Tried for the first time on a national audience, its effect was astounding. In a straightforward, President-to-people way, with no fake folksiness, he told the country its banks were now safe. Next morning tellers' windows were

Mrs. Hoover and Eleanor Roosevelt follow F.D.R. and a stony-faced President Hoover to the inauguration ceremonies.

Roosevelt takes the oath of office for the first time, March 4, 1933.

A bird's-eye view of the inauguration

Inauguration Day is a happy one for Louis Howe.

thronged with depositors bringing cash back from the mattresses and sugar bowls.

The Banking Act was passed on Thursday, March 9 (1933). On Friday, the Economy Act arrived on Congressional desks, cutting veterans' pensions and government employees' salaries. The House passed it Saturday, the Senate the following Wednesday. A week later the "Beer-Wine Revenue Act" legalized 3.2% beer. On March 31 the Civilian Conservation Corps was founded—jobs for 250,000 eighteen-to-twenty-five-year-olds in reforestation and flood control in the National Parks, under Army supervision—a true Roosevelt project.

On April 19, Roosevelt moved to devalue the overpriced dollar by taking the country off the gold standard. That sounded scary to most people but J. P. Morgan, perhaps trying to improve his image, announced that it was all right, so everyone relaxed.

For relief of the unemployed, Roosevelt asked for and got $500 million, to be distributed through states and cities. All this legislation was passed with little dissent, but next came a bill that stirred vigorous debate—the Agricultural Adjustment Act (AAA). Rex Tugwell finally sold Roosevelt on the "allotment" idea—restriction of farm production in order to raise and sustain prices. In return for voluntarily limiting his acreage each farmer would be paid a subsidy.

Never, not even in wartime, had a government in Washington made so much news. To facilitate its handling, Roosevelt introduced the live press conference. Where previously White House reporters had been brought in, given a handout, and dismissed, he invited them to crowd right up to his desk and fire questions. He had already tried out the technique in Albany and found it worked, thanks to his memory for facts, his gift for repartee, and perhaps most important, his excellent news sense—he always had a good notion of what questions would be asked.

The news flowed so abundantly that it was difficult to figure out the pattern of the New Deal's legislative program. The Banking Act was a simple bail-out of the banks by the government, drafted by Hoover's Treasury people (including Ogden Mills) and approved by William H. Woodin, new Secretary of the Treasury soon to be succeeded by Henry Morgenthau. The Economy Act gratified conservative Arizonan Lewis Douglas, the new Director of the Budget. Secretary of Agriculture Henry A. Wallace reluctantly accepted the AAA because nobody could think of anything better to protect farm prices (nobody has since). The son of a Progressive Republican farm-publishing family in Iowa that had contributed significantly to

The 1933 White House portrait of Eleanor Roosevelt

the development of hybrid corn, basis of the twentieth-century American meat-raising revolution, Wallace by an irony of fate became associated in the public mind with the slaughter of little pigs. Congress debated the AAA so long that by the time it was passed farmers in the Corn Belt had raised six million piglets. A catastrophic glut of the pork market loomed; to save the farmers from themselves Wallace was compelled to order a wholesale slaughter. Numbers of the little hams got loose in the streets of Chicago and Omaha and had to be chased down, providing unforgettable news coverage. Many people thought slaughtering baby pigs was an annual operation of the AAA.

Some of the legislation passed in the hothouse atmosphere of the New Deal had nothing to do with the Depression but was simply overdue reform that had been pigeon-holed in the years of Coolidge and Hoover. Even before the new Administration took office the old lame-duck Congress had abolished lame-duck Congresses and moved future inauguration days up to January 20. It had also passed the Twenty-first Amendment, repealing Prohibition, hereafter remembered derisively by all Democrats as "the noble experiment"—another Hoover phrase. Republican Senator George Norris, a fighting progressive from Nebraska, seized on Roosevelt's interest in public power to get his backing for the Tennessee Valley Authority. Muscle Shoals was a government-owned power project in Alabama dating back to the war, which Republican administrations had sought to sell to private power companies. It was now turned into an important national asset, a power plant which could serve as a yardstick in measuring power costs and so regulating rates, as a source of cheap power to the underdeveloped region, and—to many of the project's backers its main value—as a source of cheap fertilizer through conversion of two 1918 munitions plants.

More directly aimed at the present crisis were the establishment of the U.S. Employment Service; the Federal Securities Act, compelling full disclosure of pertinent information to innocent investors; the second Banking Act, containing a guarantee of individual deposits up to $5000 (a provision inserted by Republican Senator Vandenberg of Michigan which proved extremely successful and popular); the Farm Credit Act refinancing farm mortgages and the Home Owners' Loan Act, a godsend to both homeowners—a thousand mortgages a day were being foreclosed—and banks. But by far the most important single bill in this Niagara of legislation was the National Industrial Recovery Act.

NIRA, or NRA as it became known, was the product of different points of view—big business, anti-big business reformers, pro-labor

The banking crisis: A run on the Millbury, Massachusetts, Savings Bank

liberals, and public-works spenders. Senator Hugo L. Black of Alabama was pushing a radical thirty-hour-week bill; Henry Harriman, president of the U.S. Chamber of Commerce, and Gerard Swope of General Electric urged suspension of the anti-trust laws to permit industry-wide planning. Roosevelt finally appointed a committee representing all factions to draft a bill, telling them to "lock themselves in a room" till they had it. A common ground for many of NRA's proponents was the idea that businessmen should treat their employees reasonably and their customers ethically. This was to be achieved by codes of fair practice, to be drawn up industry by industry. The result was a blow at small businessmen, who were trying to survive the Depression by tightening the screws harder on their labor forces and cutting corners with their customers. Their squeals were drowned in a wave of patriotic, almost religious, enthusiasm; the idea of everybody promising to do his part met a national psychological need. Not only did the great bellwether in-

110

One of F.D.R.'s first acts was to declare a bank holiday.

dustries hasten to draw up codes for themselves, but industries nobody had even heard of sent representatives to Washington, proposed codes in hand. The burlesque theaters got together and wrote a code limiting themselves to four stripteases per show.

Getting the codes produced by the industries and keeping them enforced was a task Roosevelt entrusted to General Hugh S. Johnson. A retired military man with a facile pen, Johnson had written boys' adventure stories before joining the suite of Bernard Baruch, the slightly sinister, slightly comic financier who ambidextrously contributed campaign funds to both parties. Baruch probably wanted a Cabinet job; after fruitlessly backing first Governor Ritchie of Maryland and then Al Smith, he had coolly boarded the Roosevelt bandwagon with contributions that topped those of Joe Kennedy and Joe Davies, and had thrown in Johnson to help Moley write speeches. Johnson's masterpiece, delivered in Pittsburgh, was a shocking absurdity in which Roosevelt had promised to cut the federal budget by

111

25%. Glib, overbearing, bibulous, Johnson was an able, hard-driving organizer who overnight plastered the NRA's blue eagle ("We Do Our Part") on the windows of businesses across the nation. Newspapers and magazines printed it on their mastheads. NRA was a national craze, like marathon dancing.

Johnson, the codes, and the blue eagle got all the publicity. More important were the labor and public-works sections of NRA. Section 7A of the omnibus bill, put in by Frances Perkins at the suggestion of William Green, president of the American Federation of Labor, guaranteed labor's right "to organize and bargain collectively through representatives of their own choosing." Theoretically labor already had this right, but Section 7A, backed by a National Labor Relations Board to listen to grievances, swung open a gate that hard-nosed management in the heavy industries had succeeded in keeping latched.

Title II of NRA set up the Public Works Administration (PWA) for the construction of roads, bridges, sewage systems, dams, post offices, and other public civil-engineering works. It was funded with a stupendous $3.3 billion, exceeding Hoover's last total budget—so much for the Pittsburgh speech. Unfortunately PWA fell almost automatically into the lap of the Interior Department, headed by Harold L. Ickes. An old Teddy Roosevelt stalwart and Bull Moose Republican, Ickes had gone to Albany in 1932 to ask for the job of Commissioner for Indian Affairs as a reward for working for Roosevelt in the campaign. After a half hour's conversation Roosevelt had picked the burly Chicagoan to head Interior. Ickes was a good man, and in another era would have made a fine Secretary; he worked hard, took seriously his responsibility for taxpayers' money, verified the need for projects, and protected them against graft with amazing success. But what the nation needed to handle its money in 1933 was a drunken sailor. Nobody realized that; everybody patted virtuous Ickes on the back.

The "Hundred Days" (March 9 to June 16) of the New Deal came to a whirlwind close with Congressional adjournment in June, Roosevelt jauntily signing the last batch of new bills just before taking off for a vacation aboard the cruiser *Indianapolis*. It had been the most extraordinary session of Congress or beginning of an administration in the nation's history. Probably only the 1789 session of the French National Assembly could rival the New Deal in volume and significance of reform legislation.

Still making news, from the *Indianapolis* Roosevelt sent a cablegram to the just-opened London monetary conference, disassociating the United States from the attempt of gold-bloc Europeans to stabilize

A Civilian Conservation Corps camp

currencies. That was to clear the way for a monetary maneuver of his own in the fall. Henry Morgenthau had introduced him to a Cornell professor named Warren who had a plan for raising farm prices by cheapening the dollar in terms of gold. Roosevelt agreed to give it a whirl, and for several weeks the Treasury bought gold at above the world price. Farm prices rose, but slipped again; more money became available to banks for lending purposes, but there were few borrowers. The Warren experiment did no harm, but it did no good.

At this very moment a man came along with the right idea. Marriner S. Eccles, a Mormon banker from Utah, thought the conservative New York banks had too much of a stranglehold on national monetary policy. A popular, leftish writer on economics named Stuart Chase happened to hear him talking and sent him to Washington. Eccles told Rex Tugwell and through Tugwell, Roosevelt, that there was really nothing wrong with the government spending more than it took in—in fact, during a Depression, it ought to. Roosevelt listened and learned. The political poison in the recipe prevented him from really having faith, but the problem of relief

113

F.D.R. greets a reforestation worker at Camp Crottoes, Virginia, during an inspection tour of CCC camps in the Shenandoah Valley, August 12, 1933.

forced him in the right direction. The so-called Civil Works Act was a brainchild of the most fascinating New Dealer of them all, forty-three-year-old Harry Hopkins. An Iowan like Henry Wallace, Hopkins lacked the tousle-headed folksy image that made Wallace seem Midwestern and rural; Hopkins was a skinny, sallow, sharp-tongued chain smoker who liked to bet at the tracks. But he shared with Wallace a profound humanity and a lucid practicality. Joseph E. Davies described him as combining "the purity of St. Francis with the shrewdness of a race-track tout." To join the New Deal, Hopkins took a salary cut from $15,000 a year to $8000. When Roosevelt appointed him to head the first emergency relief program in the spring of 1933, Hopkins went straight from the White House to the RFC building, where he set up a desk in the hall amid piles of boxes and spent five million dollars in two hours. Hopkins did not spend

114

money foolishly; he spent it fast. His organizational talent was phenomenal. When CWA was funded in November, the problem he assumed was to brigade into useful work forces more than four million unemployed men across the nation. Within thirty days he had done it. Using some of the PWA money Ickes was so prudently conserving, Hopkins built or renovated schools, airports, roads, college buildings, state capitols across the country. Projects ranged from putting teachers back to work in Boston to restocking Kodiak Island with snowshoe rabbits. CWA spent a billion dollars, getting millions of families through a tough winter—it hit six below in Washington —and giving the economy a valuable stimulant.

But all this spending scared Roosevelt. Despite strenuous objections from progressives like La Follette, Wagner, and Bronson Cutting of New Mexico, he ordered the CWA demobilized in the spring of 1934. In a Cabinet meeting he warned that "we must not take the position that we are going to have permanent depression in this country, and it is very important that we have somebody say that quite forcefully to these people." "These people"

Norris Dam, named for Senator George Norris, a vigorous supporter of the Tennessee Valley Authority

were the unemployed; Roosevelt was expressing the great fear of Lewis Douglas and the conservatives that once you got people on the public payroll you could never get them off. He was also voicing an implication that the unemployed were themselves somehow responsible for their unemployment, a popular notion derived from grafting a long-accepted belief about the fringe unemployment of prosperous times onto the totally different mass unemployment of the Depression.

For a moment Roosevelt seized on the hope that the Depression was ending. After hitting rock bottom in the fall of 1933 the economic indicators had moved upward. But as Hopkins' spending slackened, the economy leveled off. National income for 1934 wound up well above '33, but $10 billion less than '31, and only a little over half that of '29.

At best, the New Deal had only half succeeded in bringing recovery. Its powerful, disjointed efforts reflected the unreconciled conflict between the goals of the past and the urgencies of the present. Roosevelt, who had at one moment feared the Depression might end too quickly to benefit him politically, now had to face the fact that it might last uncomfortably long. He had never quite taken seriously the idea of combatting it (though he had taken seriously the idea of helping people survive it).

Huey Long sardonically summarized the Hundred Days: "We took four hundred million from the soldiers and spent three hundred million to plant saplings." That was a more sophisticated comment than Lewis Douglas's letter to Roosevelt resigning as Director of the Budget: "Upon this [balancing the budget] . . . hangs not only your place in history but conceivably the immediate fate of western civilization." (Sara Roosevelt agreed; she told Douglas's successor that all her friends in New York wanted to know when the budget was going to be balanced.)

Getting it from both sides, and with no end to the crisis in sight, Roosevelt began to wonder if maybe the country didn't have something to fear besides fear itself.

7

Roosevelt Moves Left

FROM SHELTERED Hyde Park through elitist Groton and Harvard, and into politics from a Wall Street law office, Franklin Roosevelt had developed a social-political ideology not much different from that of thousands of other members of the educated, well-to-do class. He was strongly in favor of some fairly trivial reforms. His patriotism was excessive, but toward deep social issues his interest was dilettante. The people who in the campaign of 1920 mistook him for Teddy Roosevelt's son were not far wrong.

The Depression had appeared to him at first as a "cyclical" slowdown of the normally successful American economy—a losing streak. As it lengthened and deepened he perceived the political opportunity inherent in it, and hired Rex Tugwell mainly to supply ammunition for the Presidential campaign, observing to Tugwell, "It's a fight, and I mean a *fight*." Everything else was subordinate.

But at the very same time, listening to Tugwell and other people he became aware of the deep, mysterious sources of trouble in the American economy. Mixing the cocktails, or at the dinner table, or over the breakfast debris and morning papers, he liked to listen, then say the thing again in his own words. As his election became more certain and the Depression more ominous (despite a jolly sunburst of optimistic predictions in the press, designed to help Hoover), he could turn some attention from the "fight" to figuring out what he would do in the White House.

Fiercely opposed to the Hoover-Baruch sit-still-and-maybe-it-will-go-away line were two liberal economic doctrines which had been warring with each other for twenty years. From the beginning of his

117

candidacy through the first two years in the White House, Roosevelt heard constantly from both schools. Felix Frankfurter, a little busybody of a Harvard professor (of law, not economics) dinned the gospel according to Louis Brandeis, the aged Supreme Court liberal: the government should break up the large monopolistic corporations and enforce competition. From the rival group of liberal-left economists, represented by Tugwell, he heard the more sophisticated doctrine that bigness wasn't necessarily bad, but the government should keep a tight rein on the corporations and make them behave themselves. Both these liberal ideologies had about as much relevance to the Depression as Baruch's confidence line. Tugwell, aware of this, also espoused "pump-priming" to restore depleted purchasing power, but Tugwell, like La Follette and everyone else, was hung up on the idea that you had to raise tax revenue to pay for government spending, which automatically ruined the whole maneuver.

The world was simply not yet ready for the inventor of deficit spending, British economist John Maynard Keynes, who arrived in the United States in 1934 to improve his own economy through a lecture tour. Waspish, epicene Keynes turned off many people. He may have done the same to Roosevelt when he had tea at the White House—he afterward told Frances Perkins that he had "supposed the President was more literate, economically speaking." Keynes not only advocated spending money beyond tax revenue, but actually recommended cutting taxes while increasing spending. Every red-blooded American knew *that* was crazy.

Roosevelt was not enchanted with any of the nostrums proposed to him. Yet the year 1934 made it increasingly clear that he had to make some more moves. The men who pushed him into the course he finally took were not Keynes, Baruch, Tugwell, or Frankfurter, but four entirely different men, each of whom represented a novelty on the American political landscape. The four were Huey Long, Dr. Townsend, Upton Sinclair, and Father Coughlin.

Huey Long, senator from Louisiana, had battled vigorously for Roosevelt in Chicago and had been kept, with difficulty, at arm's length ever since. A natural-born comedian, piefaced Huey was always center stage, in straw hat, colored shirt, and rumpled white suit. "God-damn it, Franklin," he shouted, "you got to listen to me." Unruffled, Roosevelt listened, chuckled, and let Huey go his own way. But Huey had something in his Share-Our-Wealth plan. The intellectuals laughed at his proposals for guaranteed annual income, low-cost housing, and free schoolbooks, but millions of people trying to raise families on six hundred dollars a year and what they could steal weren't laughing.

In the pool of the polio foundation at Warm Springs

The Little White House, Warm Springs

Dr. Francis Townsend was an elderly Republican who had taken it into his head that old people ought to be supported by the government. His proposal was that everyone over sixty be given $200 a month. With a nice grasp of the economic implications of his plan, Dr. Townsend specified that the recipients spend their money the same month they got their hands on it, a requirement that in 1934 promised to present no problem. The intellectuals laughed again—where would all the money come from? The old

119

Louis Howe at Westport, Massachusetts

people with no jobs, no incomes, their sons and daughters in financial trouble too, didn't laugh.

Upton Sinclair was a virtuoso hack writer and insatiable do-gooder. He had burst on the national scene thirty years earlier with a novel depicting in hair-raising detail the shortcomings of the Chicago meat-packing industry. According to "Mr. Dooley," the journalistic sage of the 1900's, Theodore Roosevelt read the novel at breakfast, leaped to his feet crying, "I'm pizened!" and commenced throwing sausages out of the White House window. Sinclair had followed this triumph with many more books, most of them highly effective, all stomping on some part of the Establishment's anatomy. An immigrant Californian, he thought California a good place to begin the expropriation of big business. Summing up his program in characteristically imaginative journalese, he coined a pioneer acronym: EPIC—"End Poverty In California." When he announced his candidacy for governor in the Democratic primary, not the intellectuals but everybody laughed; when he won a smashing victory over the regular Democratic organization they stopped in mid-guffaw.

The strangest of the 1934 crop of radicals was Father Charles

120

E. Coughlin. Operating against the handicap of being a Catholic priest in Protestant, and still rather anti-Catholic, America, he captivated Protestants and Catholics alike. His charm lay in his voice. If Roosevelt's audio image was choice, Coughlin's was prime. Out of the loud speaker it rolled and reverberated, sang, and exploded. After discovering his strange power in Royal Oak, a suburb of Detroit (he was a native of Canada), Father Coughlin rapidly went national; on Sunday afternoon all over the country radios filled residential streets with his unctuous thunder. Like Huey Long he first supported the New Deal, which he characterized with typical restraint as "Christ's deal." But he capriciously broke with Roosevelt, and the cadenced invective gradually switched to the "international bankers," who gradually became more and more Jewish, and got all mixed up with the Communist International.

Heightening the radical appeal in the spring of 1934 was a natural calamity, a terrific drought which parched and blew away millions of acres of topsoil, filling the western roads with helplessly wandering

Secretary of State Cordell Hull reports to President Roosevelt after his return from the London Economic Conference.

*The candles and candleholders that surrounded Roosevelt's fifty-second
birthday cake. The celebration was at the Waldorf-Astoria.*

farm families. The AAA and other New Deal agencies moved swiftly,
but the calamity spread, feeding political grist to Long, Townsend,
Sinclair, and Coughlin.

Of the four menaces, the only one presenting an immediate problem
was Upton Sinclair, who wanted Roosevelt's backing, and as Democratic nominee, was entitled to it. But the regular Democrats,
including Farley and Howe, would sooner embrace a rattlesnake
than a socialist. Sinclair's Republican opponent, Frank Merriam,
was an old-fashioned conservative. Roosevelt's solution was summarized by press secretary Steve Early as a two-point program:
(1) Say nothing; and (2) Do nothing. It worked. All the California
tycoons, from San Francisco shipping magnates to Hollywood pro-
ducers, joined in a stupendous beat-Sinclair campaign. Merriam,
approached discreetly by a Roosevelt emissary, said publicly that
the New Deal wasn't all bad; the Democratic party organization
backed Merriam, and the specter of EPIC was laid.

122

But Sinclair's 880,000 votes (Norman Thomas had polled only a little more nationally in '32) scared Howe, Farley, and the bosses. Even the fact that the Democrats had swept everything in sight outside of California was cause for uneasiness, because it showed how slippery was the nation's slide to the left. A secret Farley poll early in 1935 revealed that Huey Long had a serious third-party capability. What if Huey worked a deal with Townsend (whose Townsend Clubs were spreading like a prairie fire) and with Coughlin, who couldn't run for President himself? It might turn the '36 election into a shambles.

Roosevelt did not panic. He had his eye on '36 as much as did Louis Howe, who was gasping out his life in Lincoln's bedroom, and Jim Farley, who was sitting in the Cabinet as Postmaster General and running the Democratic party from the Mayflower Hotel. Studying the radical opposition, Roosevelt decided to undercut it on two major fronts. In his opening address to Congress he asked for a huge public-works program funded at $4.88 billion, and a Social Security Act oriented toward the old people. The new program was attacked by conservatives in Congress, but even more loudly by liberals. La Follette wanted $9 billion for public works and even conservatives were willing to say $2 billion for direct relief, an indication of how far left the country had moved. Roosevelt's figure was moderate, and in the end accepted. Long before the money was voted, Hopkins and Ickes locked horns over how to spend it, meaning who would do the spending. Hopkins stood for "light" public works, requiring maximum unskilled labor and providing maximum unemployment relief and fastest pump-priming. Ickes stood for "heavy" or "permanent" works requiring substantial capital-goods investment but significantly improving the nation's estate—bridges, schools, sewage systems, etc. In his 1933 mood Roosevelt had favored the Ickes approach; now he switched leftwards to Hopkins. Ickes, spoiled and hurt, resigned. Roosevelt quickly kidded him out of it.

The new spending agency, christened WPA (Works Progress Administration), produced under Hopkins what an economic historian has characterized as "the most imaginatively conceived and best executed of all the New Deal recovery measures." Hopkins aimed at putting people to work doing what they did best. He had writers write (state and city guide books, many of them classics), actors act (lively Federal Theater productions), and artists paint (murals for post offices, many not bad). Even though WPA did some valuable conserving—such as saving Indiana's covered bridges— conservatives hated it.

123

Senator Wagner struck a new note with a bill designed to supplant NRA's terse 7A with a full-scale Magna Carta for labor. Roosevelt gave him no help. He did not even fight for the Social Security Act. On the contrary, his only decisive move was a personal appearance in the Capitol to lend emphasis to a strong veto message on a new soldiers' bonus bill. With all his sympathy for the veterans whose march had helped elect him, he still feared the bonus—on top of WPA it would throw the budget for a bad loss. The best he did for a new gathering of veterans in Washington was to send Eleanor out with coffee and doughnuts. (A pretty good move at that—sensible, warm-hearted Eleanor made a hit with the vets.)

Roosevelt was still trying to bat left and throw right.

Then two things happened. First, the U.S. Chamber of Commerce, at that time recognized as the voice of responsible American business, denounced the New Deal. Roosevelt was hurt—he had tried hard to please business, especially the big business represented by the Chamber of Commerce, whose president had played a large role in drafting NRA. Roosevelt had wanted the present Congress to extend NRA's two-year time limit; now he didn't know what he wanted.

Suddenly reaction dropped the second shoe. The Supreme Court declared NRA unconstitutional. The case involved a little family firm in Brooklyn that sold live chickens for kosher slaughtering. The firm ran a sweatshop and pushed diseased chickens. The facts were not in dispute. But the Court decided that the business was not interstate, even though the chickens were imported from outside New York. Worse yet, it declared that Congress lacked the power to keep diseased chickens, kosher or non-kosher, off the American dinner table.

The depth of ideological hostility to the New Deal on the part of some justices had been revealed several times (Justice McReynolds had compared Nero favorably with Roosevelt). But on the sick-chicken case the four conservatives of the Court (McReynolds, Butler, Sutherland, and Van Devanter) were joined by the two moderates (Hughes, Roberts) and even the three liberals (Brandeis, Cardozo, Stone). The absence of dissent made the decision a super-shocker.

From Wall Street to San Simeon, everybody who thought the New Deal too radical, or too egghead, or just too new, was in ecstasy. The pressure on Roosevelt was immense. The opportunity loomed to say something loud and angry. It took discipline to keep silent. Even in private he restricted himself to a well-justified demand: "Where was Ben Cardozo? Where was old Isaiah [Brandeis]?"

Eleanor's return from her trip to the Caribbean

While in the Caribbean, E.R. visits a slum at Christiansted, Virgin Islands, March 1934.

N.Y. DAILY NEWS PHOTO

Going down into a coal mine near Bellaire, Ohio, May 31, 1935.

Eleanor inspects the basement and kitchen of a homestead in Des Moines, Iowa, June 8, 1936.

Women's Day at the Century of Progress Exposition, Chicago, November 1, 1933

Finally after four days he called a press conference. When the reporters trooped in he was the picture of relaxation behind the cluttered desk—cigarette holder, big smile, not a care. Eleanor sat nearby, cozily knitting a sock. The President kidded the newsmen, asking them what was the news. A correspondent timidly inquired whether he cared to comment on the NRA decision. "That's an awful thing to put up to a fellow at this hour of the morning," he protested, and then talked for an hour and a half, expounding constitutional history with the authority of an expert. The Court, he said, had reverted to the long-discredited Knight decision (1885) on the interstate commerce clause—a "horse-and-buggy" interpretation, which made it "impossible for the Federal government to deal with national problems."

His well-reasoned objections were shot down by his enemies with the aid of the flag—the Constitution was sacred, the Court had spoken (unanimously!) and it was better for the country to go to hell observing the Constitution than to live happily in sin.

Reading such foolishness made Roosevelt really mad. People whose brains and nerve had failed, who had been reduced to muttering "budget" and "confidence" had no right to take smug pleasure in the discomfiture of a leader who had tried to lead.

Until now, he had not wanted to fight anybody. But now he saw that even the idea of trying to solve the nation's great problem had to be fought for. He picked up the cards, shuffled, and slammed down a second New Deal.

Senators and congressmen were preparing a leisurely wind-up of their profitless session, mapping vacations away from the heat and humidity. Roosevelt summoned their leaders to the White House. This time there was no jaunty cigarette holder, no smile. He pounded his fist on the desk. They could not go home, he told them, until they had passed some major legislation—in fact a brick house full. For openers, the Wagner Act (which he had not up to now even endorsed) and Social Security; then an anti-Wall Street bill to clip the wings of holding companies; finally, a new banking bill. But even that wasn't all. While the conservative opposition was reeling from these punches, it caught the wickedest uppercut of all a few days later—a tax bill that hit big incomes, both individual and corporate, that raised inheritance taxes, and that for the first time laid a hand on the "gifts" by which millionaire families had long eluded inheritance taxes. In a press conference he produced a set of facts and figures on tax evasion, or rather "tax avoidance—you hire a $250,000-fee lawyer, and he changes the word 'evasion' to 'avoidance.'"

F.D.R. had more than a million stamps in his collection.

F.D.R. and Anna set out on a sleigh ride over the grounds of the Hyde Park estate and surrounding countryside.

U.P.I.

A roar, as from so many victims of the stake, filled the editorial air. The bill was immediately dubbed "Soak the Rich," except in the Hearst papers, where it was termed "Soak the Successful." From San Simeon, Hearst wired his twenty-eight obedient editors instructions never again to employ the words "New Deal"—hereafter it was to be known to Hearst readers as the "Raw Deal."

It was a summer-long, bitter-end fight. Wagner, La Follette, and the other liberal heroes of Capitol Hill fought with their usual

129

Roosevelt signs the Social Security Act, August 14, 1935.

tenacity, but this time they had help. A stream of messages from the fronts of the several simultaneous battles poured into the White House; after each one a big hand reached for the phone and any recalcitrant or fearful congressman was coaxed, commanded, promised. The lights burned late as strategy was remapped nightly. In the end nearly all the "must" legislation was passed, though its social-economic effect was somewhat smaller than the fireworks suggested. "Soak the Rich" was modified to slightly-dampen-the-rich. Social Security, conservatively based on equal contributions from employers and employees, with nothing from the government, had the economically regressive effect of soaking the wage earner. Roosevelt knew that, but he also knew it was politically the only way.

Nevertheless, the summer's battle created an entirely fresh political alignment. Roosevelt was no longer a consensus President; instead, he was the fighting leader of the masses against conservatives and businessmen, just what Walter Lippmann said he couldn't be. Dr.

Townsend's followers gratefully accepted the "half a loaf" of Social Security (or quarter loaf—the act left many categories of old people uncovered) and Huey Long beamed his satisfaction over Soak-the-Rich: "I just want to say Amen."

Where Huey would have headed politically in the light of the Second Hundred Days, or where he could have gotten, remains a tantalizing conjecture, because that autumn a relative of an office-holder Huey had abused shot him dead in the Louisiana State House. There was nobody to fill Huey's shoes. His national movement fell into the hands of an untalented rabble-rouser named Gerald L. K. Smith, and was quickly discredited. His Louisiana political heirs made a patronage treaty with Farley to put the state back in the Democratic column ("the Second Louisiana Purchase").

Roosevelt took Hopkins and Ickes off for a fishing trip aboard the cruiser *Houston*. He had never felt better in his life. Ickes marveled at "his high cheer . . . Never did he act self-conscious" as he was carried down the companionway in the arms of two sailors to the fishing launch, where he spent every day. He returned home feeling and looking ready to take on Father Coughlin and the new Du Pont-backed "Liberty League."

Coughlin did his best to get a third-party movement going without Huey Long, but the obscure congressman (Lemke) around whom he sought to build it attracted attention only from the *Daily Worker,* which pronounced him a fascist. The Liberty League, meant to provide a rallying ground for old-line Democrats, was only a more expensive failure. It spent millions warning that the New Deal was destroying the Constitution, which was actually being twisted out of recognition by the Nine Old Men (Drew Pearson's gibe) of the Supreme Court, who threw out the AAA by 6–3 in what William Leuchtenburg calls a "wretchedly argued opinion." The Liberty League put on a boiled-shirt dinner in Washington with a national radio broadcast for its featured speaker—Al Smith. Al made a fool of himself. "There can be only one capital," he declared with raucous solemnity, "Washington or Moscow. There can be only one atmosphere of government, the clear, pure, fresh air of free America, or the foul breath of communistic Russia."

Al found that all he had done was turn himself into a Republican. If there was one identifiable group that loved Roosevelt dearly, it was the rank-and-file, party-line Democrats. They loved him for one great American reason: he was a winner.

Al's claim that Roosevelt's program was socialist drew a deeply pained reply, not from Roosevelt, but from Norman Thomas (another beautiful, though rarely heard, radio voice). Ticking off the

F.D.R. speaks from the White House portico to 4000 farmers who had gathered to voice approval of administration farm policy and to demand continuation of the AAA.

New Deal reforms one by one, the Socialist party leader identified them as conservative and capitalist. Roosevelt himself made somewhat the same point in a speech in which he employed a parable: in 1933, he said, an old gentleman wearing a silk hat fell off the end of a dock. A friend dived in and saved him, and received effusive thanks. But "today, three years later, the old gentleman is berating his friend because the silk hat was lost."

The Republicans in 1936 were lucky enough to find a good man to put up. (Herbert Hoover intimated his availability, but the GOP bosses turned green.) Alf Landon of Kansas was the only Republican governor elected west of the Mississippi in '32, and the only one in the country re-elected in '34. Another old Bull Moose Progressive, he accepted most of the New Deal reforms. But Landon was a poor campaigner in the electronic age, and all the Du Ponts'

132

A talk with North Dakota homesteaders about the drought may have provided some of the fuel for F.D.R.'s fireside chat on conservation, September 1936.

money couldn't buy him a radio voice. (To replace the Du Ponts and other millionaire deserters from the Democratic party, Farley found a new source of funds—the labor unions.)

Roosevelt and Farley managed a dramatic and effective campaign; Louis Howe, gone since April, could scarcely have improved it. The platform was no 1932 mishmash, but a proud, defiant, ringing endorsement of the New Deal. The Philadelphia convention was a monster Democratic jamboree, staged to hit a climax with Roosevelt's acceptance speech. He made it a good one. "These economic royalists complain that we seek to overthrow the institutions of America. What they really complain of is that we seek to take

The 1936 campaign in New York City

away their power." Roars not only punctuated and interrupted his phrases, they nearly drowned them. When he reached "I accept . . . ," nobody heard the rest.

That took care of the party. Away from Philadelphia, Roosevelt copied Lincoln and ran almost as a non-partisan, backing La Follette Progressives in Wisconsin, the Farmer-Labor party in Minnesota, and Republican George Norris in Nebraska. He drew astounding non-partisan and even anti-partisan support—ailing Senator Couzens of Michigan, a Republican auto millionaire, calmly threw away his own renomination to back Roosevelt. "The outcome of my own candidacy is important neither to the nation nor me," said this disinterested and truly patriotic man. In New York, Norman Thomas's Socialist party base was demolished by the defection of the Jewish garment workers, who organized the new American Labor party (father, or uncle, of the Liberal party) and nominated Roosevelt.

134

With Ickes and Wallace at Harrisonburg, Virginia, 1936.

DEAN STUDIO, HARRISONBURG, VA.

Sixty thousand people at Great Field, Atlanta, heard F.D.R. open his 1936 campaign for re-election.

U.P.I.

Overriding all political maneuverings was the fact that things were better. The economic indicators that had leveled off in early '34 had picked up under the renewed spending of '35. National income had jumped 62% over '33, from $40 billion to $65 billion (still below '29). Farm income was up 250%. Against that, Landon could make little headway, even though the Chicago *Tribune* warned its readers daily, "Only X days remain to save your country" (the *Trib*'s switchboard operators even repeated the inane message to callers), and Hearst's *Journal-American* set some kind of record by cramming into a single issue six news stories connecting Roosevelt with the Reds. The journalistic bomb of the campaign was a Moscow-supports-Roosevelt story by Donald Day, the *Tribune*'s correspondent in Riga, Latvia. The rival Chicago *Times* exposed the tale as a hoax. Hearst audaciously picked up the story to reprint before election, but somebody tipped off the White House and Steve Early torpedoed the

135

In Lincoln, Nebraska, F.D.R. delivered a speech urging the re-election of Senator George Norris as one of "the major prophets of America." October 1936.

Roosevelt and Mayor Fiorello La Guardia of New York during the 1936 campaign.

F.D.R. campaigns in Kansas City.

fabrication in a press conference. A postscript to the episode was provided nine years later in 1945, when correspondent Day was arrested for broadcasting for the Nazis.

Around Roosevelt's train and motorcade the crushes were enormous. If some people hated him, many loved him in a way few politicians get loved. Under Hoover one man had checked the White House mail, and it wasn't very good mail at that. Now fifty mail handlers were swamped, and what letters: "God bless Mr. Roosevelt and the Democratic party who saved thousands of poor people all over this country from starvation." "Your work saved our humble little home. . . . the Real Estate Business is now over 100% better than in 1932, life is 1000% better since you took Charge of our United States."

Farmers, pleased with AAA payments and further coddled by a New Deal program of rural electrification (that made few big-city headlines, but had tremendous impact), were for Roosevelt by an overwhelming margin, even in old Republican strongholds. Negroes (the ones who were allowed to vote) switched from the party that freed the slaves to the party that gave them WPA jobs. Workers in the mass-production industries, the unemployed and the employed but unorganized, flocked to the New Deal and the Wagner Act. Many small businessmen, ringing up WPA money on their cash registers, deserted the Grand Old Party. A Detroit building contractor, asked how he was going to vote, confided, "Charlie, I'm going to vote for Roosevelt as fast as I can go out the back door of the voting booth and in the front door."

The difference between Hooverism and Rooseveltism was etched deep. A New Deal official visiting his native Montana in 1934 had seen "old friends . . . men I had been to school with—digging ditches and laying sewer pipe. They were wearing their regular business suits because they couldn't afford overalls. . . . One man pulled some silver from his pocket and said, 'Frank, this is the first money I've had in my pockets for a year and a half.'" Such men were not going back to voting Republican in 1936.

In the Fireside Chats, Roosevelt came through in a way perhaps no President had before, and in a way no President, despite television, has since. In framing and delivering his talks to "the people"—the invisible, anonymous mass of America—he thought about real individuals: a farmer he knew at Hyde Park, neighbors at Warm Springs, even workmen disassembling a reviewing stand outside his window. It got through to kitchens and living rooms across the country. The effect was possibly best described by a workingman who said, "Mr. Roosevelt is the only man we ever

137

had in the White House who would understand that my boss is a son of a bitch."

A mighty tide was rising. On election eve, Jim Farley made an astounding prediction. He said that he could not see how the Republicans could carry any states except Maine and Vermont. That sounded so fantastic the press hardly even laughed at it. The *Literary Digest,* whose "straw vote" had never been wrong, pronounced Landon the winner.

Election night found the Roosevelt family gathered in Hyde Park. Tommy Corcoran, one of the best of the bright young men Professor Frankfurter had sent to Washington, played the accordion and everybody sang as they listened to state after state fall into the Roosevelt column. Some, like Pennsylvania, had not gone Democratic since the Civil War. Down in the Roosevelt Deep South country the normal Democratic majorities became nearly unanimous—91% in Mississippi, 89% in Alabama. It ended up exactly as Farley had predicted—everything except Maine and Vermont went Democratic, the biggest sweep in election history. (An ancient political adage, deriving from Maine's curious early-vote custom, "As Maine goes, so goes the nation," was destroyed by the gag, "As Maine goes, so goes Vermont.") The popular vote went to Roosevelt, 27 million to 17 million.

The *Literary Digest* died, and George Gallup, with his more scientific (if not quite infallible) sampling technique, arrived. But even Gallup wasn't as close as uncanny Farley.

Anna Roosevelt's husband, John Boettiger, answered the Hyde Park phone next day and found himself incredulously listening to Marion Davies in San Simeon. The actress and her friend William Randolph Hearst just wanted to assure everybody at Hyde Park that "there are no hard feelings at this end. . . . We know a steam roller has flattened us."

Marion was right. A steam roller had flattened Hearst and the other old-line conservative Democrats. Roosevelt's prediction to Tugwell had come true—from here on in, whatever its sins, the Democratic party offered a home to American progressives.

8

America and the Aggressors

AFTER his press conference on the sick-chicken case, Roosevelt had said nothing out loud about the Supreme Court. But with everybody in the country talking about it, not surprisingly he talked about it too, in private. The natural man for him to talk to was Homer Cummings, his Connecticut Yankee Attorney General. Cummings hated the Nine Old Men more than Roosevelt did, because every New Deal law they said was unconstitutional was one he had pronounced constitutional. To get even, Cummings cooked up a bill for Roosevelt that promised to shake up Capitol Hill, the Court, and the whole country.

They kept it secret. After an Inaugural address reminding Congress that there was a lot still to be done to make America perfect ("one third of a nation ill-housed, ill-clad . . .") and, by implication, that he couldn't do it very well with Nine Old Men on his back, he sent Cummings' bill up Pennsylvania Avenue. Basically, it called for enlarging the Court from nine to fifteen members on the pretext that the Nine needed help on their backlog of cases, and enforced retirement at seventy. Old Joe Robinson of Arkansas, Senate majority leader, was promised one of the new Court posts if he could swing the bill, or something near it. He couldn't, but he died trying, after a battle that inspired the most stupefying editorial and Congressional rhetoric of the whole New Deal. The fight ended in inglorious defeat—or did it? Roosevelt had forgotten Mr. Dooley's shrewd observation, that "the Supreme Court follows the election returns." Reading the papers, the justices had thought the country was behind their tendentious decisions; after the election they took another look at the Constitution and found that the New Deal wasn't so unconstitutional after all. While the battle still raged in Congress, the Wagner Act, Social Security, and other New Deal laws were stamped "approved." One mossback, Van Devanter, resigned, presently followed by others. As Roosevelt appointees—Black, Douglas, Murphy, Reed—slid into the vacated seats, the narrow-versus-broad interpretation pendulum was set swinging to broad, where it stuck for a long time.

But so violent were the passions aroused by the Court bill that a harmless, necessary, taxpayers'-money-saving Executive Reorganization bill was labeled the "Dictator Bill" by Father Coughlin and Hearst and killed by hysteria. (Roosevelt later got most of what he needed by a little-noticed "Executive Order," and eventually Harry Truman carried out a thoroughgoing reorganization after cleverly getting Herbert Hoover to make the recommendations.)

Yet Roosevelt's worst blunder in '37 was neither the Court fight nor the Dictator bill. It was giving in to Morgenthau's heartfelt pleas and balancing the budget. That, combined with Social Security deductions from paychecks, brought on a recession, which the press promptly blamed, not on the cutback, but on the spending. Hopkins and Ickes argued the reverse, getting support from Marriner Eccles, the Mormon Keynesian who had never read Keynes. But Morgenthau persuaded Roosevelt that it was time for the economy to "stand on its own feet," a notion which to the economic advisers of later Presidents must sound like something out of the ninth century.

The year 1937 seemed fated to be the morning-after headache for the New Deal. NRA and the Wagner Act had tardily opened the plant gates of basic industry to union organizers. A rebel faction of the sluggish AFL, led by baleful-browed John L. Lewis, made daring forays into the steel mills, auto plants, oil refineries, and rubber plants, organizing workers by the thousands. Not unnaturally, management fought. In Flint, Michigan, a bloody showdown was narrowly averted by a sensible governor (Frank Murphy); in Chicago a confrontation left ten workers dead, many wounded by uniformed Republic Steel guards.

Public sympathy should have been on the side of the workers, fighting for fundamental rights, but it wasn't. Virtually the entire American public outside organized labor not only took the opposite side, but worked itself into a steaming rage. Daily the press printed the number of man-days, or even man-hours, "lost" by strikes, a wild irony in a time when industry was running at half capacity. Side by side with that fallacy, a notion was growing that a high level of unemployment was normal.

140

F.D.R., adviser Rexford Tugwell, left, and Tugwell's assistant, W. W. Alexander, tour the PWA's large-scale housing projects, 1936.

Badgered by the correspondents to take sides on the strikes (what they meant was denounce the strikers), Roosevelt quoted Shakespeare: "A plague on both your houses." That was reasonable, but it infuriated both John L. Lewis (whose United Mine Workers had made a handsome financial contribution to the '36 campaign) and the newspapers (whose own reporters and desk men were organizing).

The commotion over strikes and the Supreme Court competed with Hitler and the Japanese for front-page space, helping to keep the country from waking up to the real danger ahead. But even without the distraction, the national mood was fatally out of phase with events. Looking back from today, after thirty years of quick-triggered American intervention in all kinds of trouble all over the globe, it is hard to believe that a generation ago Americans were so passionately determined to stay home and mind their own business. What had happened was that the imperialist intoxication of the Teddy Roosevelt-Woodrow Wilson era had ended in a "never-again" hangover. As the overdone Kaiser propaganda came into perspective, the country felt it had been played for a sucker. War debts sharpened the backlash, which peaked at just the wrong time. Hitler really was everything the newspapers had called the Kaiser, and more

F.D.R. sailed on the Indianapolis *in late November 1936 for a good-will tour of South America . . . and a rest.*

besides, but the country was too wised-up to believe it. Whatever happened in Europe, the Yanks were not coming this time, and they weren't paying any bills either. The Neutrality Acts spelled that out—France and Britain couldn't buy supplies except for cash on the barrelhead, and they had to come get the stuff themselves.

Roosevelt signed the Neutrality Acts without struggling, but he wasn't happy with them. When Japan launched its invasion of China (1937) he used Japan's insistence that it wasn't really a war to avoid applying the new law, which would have hurt China.

That wasn't enough, and he knew it. Even if 1917 was a mistake, and even if the country felt snug behind its two oceans, Roosevelt believed that America should contribute something to stopping the runaway fascist aggression.

Working with Sumner Welles, old Groton schoolmate and new Undersecretary of State, he figured out a plan. He thought if the diplomatic representatives of the world were brought together in one place they could agree on some basic principles of international conduct. The meeting might be held at sea, to avoid geographical problems, and to dramatize the global nature of the conference.

142

He presently sent the idea over to London for a judgment, but meantime ran something up the flagpole at home with a speech in Chicago. Characterizing the "international reign of terror" as an "epidemic," and warning that the Western Hemisphere would not be immune, he suggested that the peaceable 90% of the world might "quarantine" the aggressors.

Again the correspondents badgered him. How did "quarantine" square with the Neutrality Act? He fenced, refusing to go further. They concluded that the speech was some kind of trial balloon. They never did find out about the plan for a world conference. British Prime Minister Neville Chamberlain frostily thanked the American President for his "courageous initiative," but knocked down the project. Hardly concealing his view of Roosevelt as an amateur, Chamberlain suggested he leave diplomacy to experts, like Chamberlain.

The French, more realistic or more exposed than the British, were readier to accept Roosevelt's help. On the eve of Munich, Foreign Minister Bonnet suggested that Roosevelt come in and arbitrate. In the light of Wilson and T.R., the proposal did not seem far out of line, but in the phobic American mood of 1938 it was. Roosevelt had to decline the honor, leaving Munich to Chamberlain, who came home announcing that out of this nettle danger, he had plucked this flower safety. Most people agreed at first; even Roosevelt cabled tersely, "Good man." French Premier Daladier was the only immediate pessimist. But Hitler's follow-up, imposition of a brutal "protectorate" on the Czechs, proved Daladier right. When Hitler mounted a fresh diplomatic offensive, this time against Poland, all three democracies took the alarm.

Britain and France placed orders for aircraft in the United States, while Roosevelt requested appropriations for increases in the U.S. armed forces. Harold Ickes' PWA had already contributed to the Navy's yards and ships, including the big aircraft carriers *Enterprise* and *Yorktown*. Now Roosevelt called for more ships of all types, and 2000 aircraft a month. In January 1939 one of the newest types, a Douglas A-20, crashed in California. The pilot was killed and a French air force officer was injured. That stirred an outcry —what was a Frenchman doing in an American airplane? No sooner did the furor subside than a new one was created by a report that Roosevelt had said America's frontier was on the Rhine. That was the truth, but nobody wanted to hear it. Roosevelt hastily denounced the report.

He tried another novel diplomatic move, notes to Hitler and Mussolini listing thirty-one countries which he asked them to agree

143

His hand on a rain-spattered, cellophane-covered old family Bible, F.D.R.
took his second oath of office from Chief Justice Hughes, January 20, 1937.

not to invade. The dictators laughed in his face, going so far as
to get some of the listed countries to state that they did not feel
threatened. Within two years every single one of them was either
occupied or trembling. But what the world was struck by at the
time was the feebleness of the American gesture. Twenty years
after Woodrow Wilson arbitrated the world's great issues in Paris,
America was a self-made bystander.

Europe, shifting for itself, did it badly; London, Paris, and Moscow
failed to get together, and Hitler cleverly seized the opportunity to
seduce Stalin. At 3 A.M. of September 1 (1939), Roosevelt's bedside phone rang. It was Ambassador Bullitt in Paris. German
troops had invaded Poland, bombs were falling on Warsaw. Roosevelt grimly hung up and ordered the news relayed to all Navy
ships and Army posts.

Britain and France showed how far out of date they were with
their formal declarations of war, just like old times. But the Allies'
declarations (or at least Britain's—U.S. Wasps had little use for
France) brought a flip-flop in the mainstream of U.S. public opinion

144

that dwarfed the flip-flop done by the little American Communist Party after the Nazi-Soviet pact. When Roosevelt gave his Fireside Chat, he told his audience that unlike Wilson in 1914, he could not "ask that every American remain neutral in thought."

With England at war, a Gallup poll showed an astounding 44% suddenly prepared to ship U.S arms if a German victory threatened, never mind about the Neutrality Act or the war debts, or even getting paid. Herbert Hoover, arguing against a revision of the Neutrality Act to benefit the Allies, said there was no danger of German victory and nobody should worry about it (ten years earlier he had predicted prosperity around the corner).

What Hoover wanted people to worry about was the possibility that the war in Europe might provide a pretext for Roosevelt to run for a third term. Almost since the '36 election some Democrats had been talking third term—New Deal bureaucrats looking out for their jobs, big-city bosses looking out for their power, and people all through the country who had come to trust Roosevelt and didn't want him to leave. Roosevelt had at one time groomed Harry Hopkins as his successor, but Hopkins' operation for stomach cancer finished that. Among the eager volunteers now straightening ties in front of mirrors, the most prominent were Vice-President Garner, Secretary of State Cordell Hull, and Jim Farley. Garner was seventy-one, Hull sixty-eight, and Farley devoid of experience in government except as Postmaster General. Yet Garner and Farley busily lined up delegates, while Hull, who viewed delegate-hunting as infra dig for a Secretary of State, counted on Roosevelt's blessing.

However agreeable Roosevelt found the power of the Presidency, he almost surely would have bidden it a reluctant good-by if the war had gone well for the Allies. But in the spring of 1940 the bedside telephone and the cable brought one shock after another. As Hitler's dive-bomber–tank–88-gun combination hit Denmark and Norway, Netherlands, Luxembourg, and Belgium, and burst into France, Lloyd George's pithy comment, "Too little and too late," sounded as valid a critique for America as for Britain and France. De Gaulle's "France has lost a battle, but has not lost a war," also had application—America had lost a battle before even finding itself in a war.

American thinking, turned halfway around the previous September, now completed 180 degrees. The first day of the German offensive in the West (May 10, 1940), General Marshall, a cool VMI alumnus whom Roosevelt had promoted over several stuffy West Pointers to chief of the general staff, requested a large expansion of the Army. On May 16, the day after the Dutch surrender and the retreat of

145

With the Cabinet in March 1937, clockwise from left: Henry Morgenthau, Treasury; Homer S. Cummings, Attorney General; Claude Swanson, Navy; Henry A. Wallace, Agriculture; Frances Perkins, Labor; John Nance Garner, Vice-President; Daniel C. Roper, Commerce; Harold L. Ickes, Interior; James A. Farley, Postmaster General; Harry H. Woodring, War; Cordell Hull, Secretary of State.

the RAF to England, Roosevelt and Marshall upped the aircraft goal from 24,000 to 50,000 a year. In the midst of Dunkirk, Marshall decided he now needed an army of two million, which automatically meant an unheard-of, un-American peacetime draft. Billions were voted by congressmen who had battled government spending for years. An Office of Emergency Management was hastily created to handle the pell-mell procurement program.

On June 15, the day after the fall of Paris, Roosevelt authorized Dr. Vannevar Bush, president of the Carnegie Institute, to mobilize U.S. scientists in a search for new weapons, including the possibilities that might lie in "the fission of uranium." Addressing a businessmen's group he warned that "the buffer has been the British fleet and the French army"—putting the American frontier on the Rhine

146

F.D.R. is greeted by Rev. Howard S. Wilkinson, left, as he and Eleanor leave services at St. Thomas Episcopal Church in Washington, March 1937.

The Du Ponts and Roosevelts were linked in 1937 when Franklin, Jr., married Ethel du Pont on June 30.

after all. A Gallup poll showed only 35% believing the United States could stay out of the war.

New British Prime Minister Winston Churchill (Chamberlain was the first casualty of May 10) confidentially cabled an urgent request for fifty recently mothballed U.S. destroyers. On June 4, just after Dunkirk, he spelled out his view of the future: "We shall defend

Members of the International Ladies Garment Workers Union gather around the President after a private White House performance of the revue, "Pins & Needles," March 3, 1938.

Mayor La Guardia and Representative Caroline O'Day of New York get a special tour of F.D.R.'s new "Hilltop Cottage" at Hyde Park, August 27, 1938.

The sight of the Presidential yacht Potomac *leaving the harbor always drew crowds. On Navy Day 1938, the President and his party leave for a tour of the Navy Yard.*

our island," he promised, "we shall never surrender . . . ," but getting to the point, the headquarters of the British Empire might be moved to Canada "until, in God's good time, the New World, with all its power and might, steps forth to the rescue and the liberation of the Old." French Premier Reynaud desperately asked for large-scale American aid to carry on the war from North Africa; taken aback, Roosevelt promised arms in "constantly increasing quantity," but he knew better than anybody that American production was scarcely started.

As the Battle of France gave way to the Battle of Britain, and America's emotional involvement jumped a couple of orders of magnitude, Roosevelt faced the dilemma of Churchill's frankly importunate plea for destroyers. Britain was more or less invasion-proof, but it was far from blockade-proof. Though Roosevelt wanted badly to help, it wasn't easy. One country doesn't just hand over fifty warships to another country, no matter how much it loves it, or what the danger is. There had to be a quid pro quo. The idea for one was supplied by a hawk group called the Century, who were an outgrowth of William Allen White's Committee to Keep America Out of War by Aiding the Allies. The Century Group, which included future Secretary of State Dean Acheson, ex-Director of the Budget Lewis Douglas, and playwright Robert Sherwood, proposed that the United States swap the mothballed destroyers for

149

air-sea bases in British possessions in the Western Hemisphere. The bombs falling on London put the thing over with the public (bombs had fallen before, but only on people like the Chinese, so nobody had noticed much). Roosevelt secretly extracted a pledge from Churchill that if Britain were invaded the British fleet (whose possible surrender to Hitler Churchill had used as a threat back in May) would be sent to Canada. A secret military arrangement was worked out with Canada at the same time.

The Churchill deal could not help giving Roosevelt satisfaction. Those elderly destroyers were there because he had pushed the navy-second-to-none thing back in 1917. And the deal itself, no matter how you looked at it, was a great one—so one-sided that Churchill, cornered though he was, quibbled.

The blitz made Roosevelt's third-term candidacy a certainty, leaving several unavoidable bruises. Garner was the first to get his lumps. Unable to conceal his distaste for the New Deal in Cabinet meetings, he had also failed to hide his anti-labor maneuvers in the Senate. John L. Lewis, wonderful old Shakespearean ham with eyebrows to rival Garner's, set a committee hearing on its ear by characterizing the V.P. as "a poker-playing, whisky-drinking evil old man . . . whose knife is ever searching, searching, searching for the pulsing heart of labor." The outraged Texas delegation caucused to draft a reply but ran into a slight problem—one member, young Congressman Lyndon Johnson, wouldn't go along, pointing out that after all, it was true. When Garner publicly announced his candidacy Roosevelt told some of the Cabinet, "I see Garner has tossed his bottle into the ring." Lewis said later that he had deliberately set out to wreck Garner's candidacy. In any case, several Roosevelt slates clobbered Garner slates in primaries, which pretty well wiped out the Texan. That left Hull and Farley. Hull was a faithful, if not exactly brilliant New Deal liberal, who had been born in a log cabin—what more could you ask? But since he had no delegates he could hardly get the nomination unless Roosevelt anointed him.

Things stood at that point when the Republican convention opened in Philadelphia. On its eve Roosevelt executed a consummate maneuver. He brought two prominent, highly respected Republicans into the Cabinet in the two defense posts. As Secretary of War he recruited wispy, Ivy League, World War I Major Henry L. Stimson, who as Secretary of State under Hoover had opposed Japanese aggression in Manchuria. As Secretary of the Navy, Roosevelt brought in ex-Rough Rider Frank Knox, publisher of the internationalist-minded Chicago *Daily News* and Republican Vice-Presidential candidate in 1936. Knox was a good second choice

*While on a Caribbean cruise in 1939, F.D.R. conferred
with Admirals William D. Leahy and C. C. Bloch.*

after Alf Landon turned down the bid—Landon, who approved
Roosevelt's foreign policy as he did his domestic policy, believed
in the two-term tradition and made Roosevelt's withdrawal a condition of entering the Cabinet.

The Republicans had a problem finding a candidate. The best
the regulars could think up was either young Tom Dewey, able
and ambitious, but only a D.A. despite the glamour of sending
New York racketeers to the chair, or Robert Taft, scion of a Presidential family and no bad politician, but only a just-elected junior
senator. Into the vacuum flowed a mass of frustrated Republican
party enthusiasm to congeal around the original Madison Avenue
candidate, Wendell L. Willkie. Willkie was a power company executive who felt his firm had had its toes stepped on by TVA.
To his innocent surprise he found the *Saturday Evening Post* re-
ceptive to complaining articles by him. Taking note of his rumpled
good looks, ambition, and hatred of Roosevelt, a couple of Henry
Luce editors successfully promoted his candidacy. Their attempt
to emphasize his Indiana small-town background was flattened by one

punch-line from Ickes: "He's just a simple, barefoot Wall Street lawyer." Like Landon, Willkie suffered from forensic weakness. In his case it was hoarseness aggravated by a penchant for the arm-waving cliché—"the greatest crusade in the history of the world!" (his candidacy, that is).

A competent candidate and a well-run campaign might have beaten Roosevelt in 1940. The Republicans had scored successes in the 1938 off-year election, possibly abetted by an ill-advised Roosevelt attempt to "purge" several conservative Democrats in the primaries. That move, urged by some of his younger hotheads, had added fuel to the dictatorship charge. And the two-term tradition certainly carried weight with most Americans. The world was full of dictatorships and nobody was very sure how those things got started. Willkie clumsily knocked down his best issue in advance by accepting the nomination with the fatuous demand, "Bring on the champ!"—in other words, challenging the Democrats to nominate Roosevelt.

Shirt-sleeved reporters toss questions at Roosevelt, who was visiting Warm Springs in April 1939 with Secretary of Commerce Harry Hopkins.

The opening of the World's Fair in New York and the state visit of
King George and Queen Elizabeth of Great Britain in June were two
moments of peace and tranquillity in 1939.

Christmas at the White House in 1939

Roosevelt was ready to pick up the challenge, but the mechanics of getting the nomination were awkward. He wanted to be drafted, and he wanted the draft to be genuine. How could he explain that to Hull and Farley?

Hull proved too gentlemanly to be difficult. Roosevelt invited him to lunch at the White House and complained about all the pressure being put on him to run, touching lightly on Hull's possible shortcomings as a candidate—from the South, sixty-eight years old, not a big labor favorite. Hull got the message. That left Farley. For Farley, the fall of France, the menace to Britain, the danger to the United States were irrelevant. What was relevant was the rules of the game—Roosevelt had had his two terms, now he should step aside and let Farley loose in the Chicago hotels.

Roosevelt invited Farley to Hyde Park for the weekend. The two pros went through a family lunch at which Sara, who had

F.D.R. presided over the first goldfish bowl drawing of selective service registrants while Secretary of War Henry L. Stimson drew the first capsule. Below, Roosevelt signs the bill.

grown fond of being the mother of the President, urged Farley to help her son get re-elected. (Eleanor, on the other hand, was firmly opposed to the third term.) They posed for the photographers before squaring off in the study for an eyeball-to-eyeball confrontation. It was hot, and the two big men took off their coats. Roosevelt tried a little snow. "Jim, I don't want to run and I'm going to tell the convention so."

"If you make it specific, the convention will not nominate you," said unsmiling Jim. He went on to add that a third term was not a nice thing, and when Roosevelt asked what Farley would do in his place Farley recommended the words of General Sherman.

Roosevelt, who had to be aware that he was putting his life on the line in going for another four years of pressure, gripped the arm of his chair, drew on his cigarette, and said earnestly, "Jim, I could not in these times refuse to take the inaugural oath, even if I knew I would be dead in thirty days."

They got onto the Vice-Presidency. Farley as good as admitted that he was maneuvering for the Number Two spot behind Hull. If behind Hull, why not behind Roosevelt? But Roosevelt quickly parried that too. Farley hardly grasped the meaning of Roosevelt's frank allusion to his affliction: "There is no telling how long I can hold out. You know, Jim, a man with paralysis can have a breakup any time. . . . It's essential that the man who runs with me should be able to carry on." He didn't mean just physically; he meant carry on the New Deal tradition in the Democratic party —something beyond Farley's capacity. With Hopkins sidelined, Roosevelt had mentally picked Henry Wallace. Farley warned him that Wallace would "handicap the ticket in the East"—translation, would scare off contributions.

Farley went away mad, which set up the problem in Chicago. Who would organize Roosevelt's draft? Mayor Kelly, an old sanitary engineer, stepped in with an unforgettable Chicago creation, "the voice from the sewer." As Senator Barkley read a message from Roosevelt that he had no desire to continue in office, that the convention should feel free, etc., the PA system suddenly broke out in a single-throated roar: "We want Roosevelt!" It was a machine-made copy of the "We want Willkie" which had stampeded the Republican convention. The voice was that of Tom McGarry, Mayor Kelly's leather-lunged superintendent of sewers, who was sitting in the basement of the hall with a mike wired into the PA system overhead. Delegates poured into the aisles, the demonstration swept Farley and the others under the seats, Roosevelt was nominated for the unprecedented, if well-prepared, third term. Harry Hopkins,

THE MEN
AROUND THE PRESIDENT

U.P.I.

Vice-President John N. Garner and F.D.R. share a joke at the annual Jackson Day dinner in 1940.

U.P.I.

At ground-breaking ceremonies for the new $80-million New York-Brooklyn tunnel are Sen. Robert Wagner (rear), Sen. James Mead, F.D.R., Gov. Herbert Lehman, and Mayor Fiorello La Guardia.

Senator Alben Barkley, left, and Postmaster General James Farley relax with the President at Jefferson Island, Maryland, in 1937.

U.P.I.

Col. Frank Knox was appointed Secretary of the Navy in July 1940.

In the summer before the 1940 election, with Vice-Presidential candidate Henry Wallace at Hyde Park.

Josephus Daniels on the grounds of the Washington Monument at the National 4-H Camp, 1940

Campaign 1940

playing the Louis Howe role, successfully put Wallace over for V.P. despite the strenuous opposition of the bosses.

The campaign was one of America's strangest. In September the isolationists organized the "America First Committee" (the "America Next Committee," Ickes labeled it) to counter the White Committee to Aid the Allies. Most of the White Committee were moderate conservatives like Henry Luce, while America First brought together strange bedfellows—General Wood, Colonel McCormick, Robert Hutchins, Norman Thomas, Charles Lindbergh. But the two committees represented only the two extremes of opinion on the war; the majority of the country was schizophrenically split on saving Britain and staying out. Roosevelt was a prisoner of that vast popular indecision. So was Willkie. The best he could do with the war issue was to endorse Roosevelt's aid to Britain while swearing holes through pewter pots that only a vote for Willkie would keep American boys out of foxholes.

Roosevelt sat out the first half of the campaign, letting Willkie wear out his novelty and his voice (reading about his rival's throat problem, Roosevelt told his doctor, Ross McIntire, to help Willkie's doctors—"We've got to keep him talking"). Finally he hit back with a series of well-prepared speeches—Hopkins had recruited Robert Sherwood to fill disaffected Moley's role. Roosevelt successfully hung anti-preparedness on the Republicans in Congress, but went over-

160

BETTER
A 3rd. TERMER

THAN A
3rd. RATER!

*Greeting the crowds in his home territory, Newburgh, New York,
and (below) going to vote with Eleanor and his mother, 1940*

board in response to pleas from the bosses on keep-American-boys-out-of-foreign-wars. In Boston he reiterated the theme, and promised to say it *again* and *again* and *again,* with the archaic New England pronunciation lending unhappy emphasis. Looking back afterward, both Roosevelt and Willkie must have wished they had been a little more restrained. Their mutual straddling stance was a bad enough reflection on American democracy, without their categorical disclaimers, which both of them knew could not be fully valid.

Seated before his table of charts at Hyde Park, Roosevelt was more concerned about the returns than in '32 or '36, but they were reassuring from the start. When Connecticut, an early bellwether, fell into the Roosevelt column, he broke out in his victory smile. By midnight it was all over and he was on the front porch addressing the neighbors. Everybody was happy, though Sara had a slight qualm. "A lot of my friends and relatives are not going to like this," she told Grace Tully.

9

The Crisis Year

To WIN the war, as everybody wanted him to, and to keep American soldiers safe at home, as everybody also wanted, Roosevelt proposed the Lend-Lease program to Congress. Explaining it to the public, he hit on a delightfully homely metaphor in his Fireside Chat: what should a man do whose neighbor's house has caught fire? Why, he should lend his garden hose, free, and after the fire is out he can take it back. That got nicely around the matter of Britain's World War I debt and the even stickier question of figuring out what kind of funds Britain had available in the United States in 1941. In a more ringing phrase, Roosevelt called for expanding production to turn America into an "arsenal of democracy," an arsenal being something that supplies weapons but does no fighting itself.

Winston Churchill solemnly endorsed the arsenal theory. "We do not need [the American army] this year, or next year, or any year that I can foresee," he stated.

Not everybody believed that; liberals like Senators La Follette (son of Fighting Bob) and Wheeler, conservatives like Lindbergh and McCormick, and 72% of the Gallup poll thought the United States was headed for war. But where the public broke ranks with the isolationists was that 60% of Gallup's people thought it was more important to aid Britain than to avoid war. The strongest sentiment for war was in the South (did the pollsters interview whites only, or did Southern blacks echo white sentiments?), a fact which gave Roosevelt a reunited Democratic party and made it impossible for the isolationists to defeat Lend-Lease (passed March 11, 1941).

The best argument the opposition thought up was that Roosevelt might take it into his head to send American arms to Russia. But a spring of disaster for Britain in Greece and Africa turned that argument right around. When Hitler launched his invasion of Russia (June 22, 1941), Americans rallied patriotically to the Kremlin. The top military men of both Washington and London were elated, within limits—their unanimous opinion was that it would take from three weeks to three months for the Germans to polish off the Russians, and then it would take six more weeks to move the German army back to the Atlantic coast from Siberia—probably too late for good invasion weather in the Channel.

Churchill, well-informed on American public opinion, thought that he could use the Russian interlude to talk Roosevelt into a declaration of war. He proposed a face-to-face meeting. Roosevelt agreed, though he perceived Churchill's intentions. He sent Harry Hopkins, who had switched from Number One spender to Number One warmonger, to London to set up the meeting. In London, Hopkins had an impulse. Getting passage on an RAF flying boat, he took off for Moscow via Archangel. For frail Hopkins, living on borrowed time, the trip was an excruciating trial, but it produced a major result. In a talk with Stalin in the Kremlin he got surprisingly frank facts and figures on the fighting front and on Russian production, as well as a long list of Russian Lend-Lease needs starting with AA guns and aluminum for Russian aircraft factories. The net impression which Hopkins conveyed back to Roosevelt was that the Russians intended to fight quite a little longer than three months.

Casually quitting Washington (August 3, 1941) for a "vacation cruise" off Maine in the Presidential yacht *Potomac,* Roosevelt switched secretly to the cruiser *Augusta,* which in company with the battleship *Arkansas* and the cruiser *Tuscaloosa,* carrying the brass, sailed north to a secret rendezvous at Argentia, Newfoundland, one of the new Navy bases acquired in the destroyer deal. The other party to the rendezvous was H.M.S. *Prince of Wales.* The fact that Roosevelt came in a cruiser and Churchill in a battleship was symbolic—Churchill, prime minister of a nation at war, was the senior partner, above all in his own eyes. He brought along a much larger retinue of brass than Roosevelt, including a full press complement, disguised as Ministry of Information bureaucrats. U.S. air chief Hap Arnold hastily sent Elliott Roosevelt off to get a Signal Corps photographer. Elliott, a captain in the Air Corps whose commission had inspired vast sarcasm from the Republican press, and Franklin, Jr., an ensign in the Navy, were present by Presidential order; the night before Churchill's arrival they had the first of several happy war-

Following his third-term election, Roosevelt had a chance to fish and catch up on sleep on a much needed cruise aboard the Tuscaloosa.

A group of men gather intently around the radio in a 42nd Street pool hall in New York to listen to the President.

time reunions. About the next day's meeting, Roosevelt told his sons, "Watch and see if the P.M. doesn't start off by demanding that we immediately declare war on the Nazis."

After lunch in the captain's cabin of the *Augusta,* Churchill spoke. "My information, Franklin [it was "Mr. President" with other officials present, but "Franklin" in private, from the very start], is that the temper of the American people is strongly in our favor. That in fact they are ready to join the issue."

Roosevelt parried with a suggestion that Churchill read some of the Congressional Record on the Lend-Lease debate. But at dinner that night Churchill poured it on. Reviewing the war, with vivid descriptions of all the battles, he occupied the stage, reducing Roosevelt, normally the star of his own dinner table, to the role of supernumerary. Working up to a peroration, the British leader exclaimed to the American, "You've got to come in beside us! If you don't declare war, declare war, I say, without waiting for them to strike the first blow, they'll strike it after we've gone under, and their first blow will be their last as well!"

Roosevelt brought up the Russians, whose resistance to invasion was making headlines.

But for the Russians, Churchill had only contempt. "When Mos-

166

Bestowing the "Outstanding Airman of the World" award for 1939 on Alexander P. de Seversky, an articulate proponent of preparedness in the air.

cow falls . . . As soon as the Germans are beyond the Caucasus . . . When Russian resistance finally ceases . . ." And once more, not only should the bulk of Lend-Lease be earmarked for Britain, but "You must come in, if you are to survive!"

In the military discussions the next day, King, Marshall, and Arnold had to argue strenuously with their British counterparts over Lend-Lease to Russia. But they stuck to their point, and that night at dinner the balance of power showed signs of shifting. Roosevelt began pressing Churchill on such touchy matters as liberation for colonial peoples, aid to underdeveloped regions, and free trade after the war. Churchill hit back with a "What about the Philippines?" but Roosevelt had a good answer—the Philippines were assured by act of Congress of independence in 1946. Churchill began to cavil, and soon regained command of the meeting, or at least of the conversation. But Roosevelt had done what he sought to do: make freedom for India, Burma, and other colonial countries an Anglo-American issue. Next day the "Atlantic Charter," hastily improvised by Sumner Welles, papered over the ideological split with generalities (among which Welles forgot to include that old American standby, freedom of religion, causing conservatives afterward to suspect a Communist plot). At the final dinner, with only Hopkins and the two Roosevelt

167

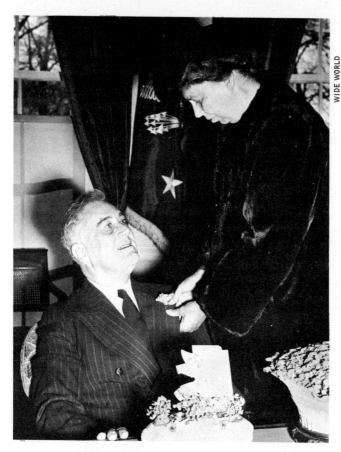

In honor of both St. Patrick's Day and their 36th wedding anniversary in 1941, the First Lady pins a gree carnation on her husband's lapel.

boys present, Churchill got around to the subject of Empire once more, but with a new note. "Without America," he conceded (according to Elliott), "the Empire won't stand."

Churchill's concern about the Empire was immediate—he had strong apprehensions about the menace from Japan, and urged Roosevelt to tell Tokyo that any move against British Malaya or the Dutch East Indies (Indonesia) would mean war with the United States. Roosevelt turned him down on that too, saying that he thought he could "baby the Japs along" for another three months.

But though he resisted Churchill on immediate war against Germany and immediate showdown with Japan, Roosevelt privately agreed by now that America's entrance was desirable and unavoidable. As Admiral Stark said, given as a national goal the saving of Britain, "ultimately . . . we have to enter the war." For the time being, America could continue to build up the arsenal of democracy while the German army was tied up in Russia (Stalin was just as eager as Churchill for an American declaration of war), and while Roosevelt "babied the Japs." But the string was going to run out sometime, either in the South Pacific or in Russia.

168

The $350,000 Roosevelt Library at Hyde Park was dedicated in June 1941.

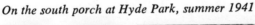

On the south porch at Hyde Park, summer 1941

At first it seemed as if war were coming the same way as in 1917, via the U-boats. Roosevelt had pressed Hitler hard already by occupying Greenland and Iceland. One inevitability led to another— if U.S. Navy ships convoyed British cargoes to Iceland, they were sure to become U-boat targets, and if they were exposed to getting hit, they had to be able to shoot on sight to protect themselves. In the deep-sea skirmishing, a U.S. destroyer was near-missed, then one

169

"At last we've gotten together," said Roosevelt as he and Winston Churchill met for the Atlantic Charter Conference. Churchill greets Franklin, Jr., and (below) attends religious services.

was hit, then one (the *Reuben James*) was sunk. The country was a whisker away from war, yet still not quite there.

On the other front, Japanese Premier Prince Konoye tried to arrange a summit conference with Roosevelt (November 1941). But he made it clear that the price of the summit was cessation of U.S. aid to China. Much as Roosevelt wanted to baby Tokyo, he couldn't abandon China. Nobody, from the hawks who had taken over the White Committee to the nationalists who had taken over America First, would stand still for that. In Tokyo, dovish Konoye resigned in favor of superhawk Tojo, who outlined a new, last-resort, diplomatic offensive for Ambassador Nomura in Washington. U.S. Intelligence, which had long enjoyed amazing success in breaking Japanese codes, gave Roosevelt and Hull the facts well in advance. Tojo had two plans, Plan A and Plan B. Plan A called for the United States to acquiesce in a two-year Japanese occupation of all China and a permanent position of dominance for Japan in East Asia. Tojo could hardly hope to get anywhere with that one. Plan B called for cessation of U.S. aid to China and resumption of normal trade with Japan, meaning oil shipments, which Roosevelt had cut off. That was so close to what Konoye had proposed that the answer seemed foregone, which gave tantalizing interest to something else the codebreakers reported: Admiral Yamamoto's orders to the fleet to prepare "Operation One"—now what could that be?

To help Nomura present his two plans, Tojo sent another envoy, Kurusu. When on November 26, 1941, Hull (and Roosevelt) turned down Plan B, they offered a counter-proposal—a non-aggression treaty. That was a plain stall, and warnings were sent out to Admiral Kimmel in Hawaii and to MacArthur in the Philippines that war was imminent. An exchange between Tokyo and Berlin was also decoded—Tojo turned down a German bid to join in the war against Russia and instead extracted a Hitler promise to declare war on the United States if Japan did.

On Saturday, December 6, a cable came from Ambassador Winant in London marked "Triple Priority," and "Personal and Secret to the President and Secretary." It reported that the British had spotted two large Japanese convoys off Indochina, headed south. Roosevelt and Hull decided on an appeal directly to Emperor Hirohito to try to warn Japan off the evident intention of invading Malaya or the Dutch Indies. Hull drafted a message and sent it to the White House. By then it was late afternoon; Roosevelt caught Grace Tully just as she was leaving her office. Dictating a few changes in Hull's draft, he had Grace type it up and rush it back to the State Department for transmission to Ambassador Joseph Grew in Tokyo.

171

A solemn President addressed the Joint Session of Congress and the nation on December 8, 1941, and (below) signed the declaration of war against Japan.

Harry Hopkins, who had been living for some time in Louis Howe's (and Lincoln's) old room, came in and they discussed the situation over dinner. At 9:30 a naval aide suddenly brought a new message—a freshly decoded cable from Tokyo to Nomura in Washington. Roosevelt read it through and handed it to Hopkins. Its implication was fairly clear—that a Japanese offensive move was imminent. But there was no clue as to where the blow would fall. Roosevelt and Hopkins (as well as Hull, Marshall, and Stark) still assumed it would be against Malaya, the Dutch Indies, or possibly the Philippines. Hopkins said it was tough that the initiative had to be left to the Japanese—since it appeared certain they meant to bring on war, it was too bad "we can't strike the first blow and so prevent surprise." But Roosevelt said, "No, we can't do that. We are a democracy and a peaceful people."

The next day Hopkins returned to the Oval Room for lunch. Until a reply was received to Roosevelt's message to Hirohito, or until Japanese landings were reported in Malaya or wherever, there was nothing to discuss, and their talk this time was "far removed from war." The two had a plan they liked to kick around for a fishing lodge in Florida after the war—Roosevelt had even drawn a sketch of the place.

Their rambling talk was interrupted at 1:40 by the telephone. It was Navy Secretary Knox. The Navy had picked up a radio signal from the commander in chief at Pearl Harbor that an air raid was on and *"this is no drill."*

Hopkins could not believe it: "Surely Japan would not attack in Honolulu!" Roosevelt was a little less incredulous.

From the military point of view, "Air raid on Pearl Harbor" did not at first sound especially ominous. By the time the bad news started coming in, Knox, Stimson, Marshall, Hull, and the military and naval aides had arrived in the Oval Room. Admiral Stark telephoned a stream of reports from the Navy Department which Grace Tully took down in shorthand and transcribed by typewriter while everyone crowded around reading over her shoulder. Shocked disbelief gave way to fury. "The Boss," according to Grace, "maintained greater outward calm than anybody else but there was rage in his very calmness. With each new message he shook his head grimly and tightened the expression of his mouth."

A telephone connection was established to Governor Poindexter in Honolulu. As Roosevelt questioned him the governor's voice suddenly rose; turning to the group, Roosevelt exclaimed, "My God, there's another wave of Jap planes over Hawaii right this minute!"

For the third time, Franklin Roosevelt took the Presidential oath of office at the Capitol.

The Navy had never quite taken seriously the potential of aircraft against battleships, Billy Mitchell notwithstanding. In a way, that was no wonder, because Japan's strike at Pearl Harbor was the war's first big carrier task-force mission. The Navy got off rather well, considering, owing to the lucky accident that the two big U.S. carriers were out on patrol (they didn't find the enemy, but the enemy didn't find them either), and to the fact that most of the sunken battleships could be raised off the shallow bottom. Besides, it turned out that battleships were not good for much anyway.

But at the moment the catastrophe seemed overwhelming. Roosevelt called a Cabinet meeting for that evening, and asked the Congressional leaders to come to the White House.

Meantime, at five o'clock he called Grace into the Oval Room. He was alone at his desk, on which were stacked the messages of disaster. He was lighting a cigarette, and took a deep drag before speaking. "Sit down, Grace," he said. "I'm going before Congress tomorrow. I'd like to dictate my message. It will be short."

He took another puff and began dictating "in the same calm tone in which he dictated his mail." Only this time he took special pains, even inserting the punctuation:

"Yesterday comma December Seventh comma Nineteen forty-one dash a date which will live in infamy dash . . ."

10

Dr. Win-the-War

A LARGE REASON for Roosevelt's and everybody's astonishment at Japan's attack was that the attack was so stupid. By an irony the Japanese deserved, Hitler chose December 7 to admit defeat before Moscow, making it look as if Tojo had gone far out of his way to join the losers.

From America's point of view, a few battleships were well sunk if they united the country, and Pearl Harbor united the country as nothing else could have. Senator Wheeler and the other isolationists whipped off their coats and roared for a fight to the finish. Roosevelt welcomed most of them home, no matter what names they had called him. But not quite all of them. Captain Joe Patterson, another old Groton schoolfellow and boss of the nation's largest newspaper, the New York *Daily News,* had at first been Roosevelt's strongest press supporter. The *News* had raised money by public subscription to build the White House swimming pool for Roosevelt's exercise. But Patterson had followed his relatives, Colonel McCormick in Chicago and Cissy Patterson in Washington, into a blind and virulent isolationism which saw Hitler as no danger and Roosevelt as some kind of a traitor. When Patterson arranged to come in and make friends Roosevelt invited him to sit down, then produced a set of clips of *News* editorials, which he proceeded to read aloud. When he unsmilingly asserted that the *News* had aided America's enemies, the Captain broke down and cried.

Like many penitents, Captain Patterson wept but did not reform. Along with some other isolationists and Roosevelt-haters (two groups that overlapped but did not coincide) he merely adjusted his weaponry. Roosevelt rolled skillfully with the chief thrust of the post-Pearl Harbor opposition. At his press conference he came up with another homely metaphor: Dr. New Deal, he said, was out for the duration, replaced by Dr. Win-the-War. No more harassment of business; on the contrary, lots of juicy war orders, for everybody from GM and GE down to the Seventh Avenue foreman opening a shirt factory in Mississippi. It looked like a wonderful war. As far as winning it went, good old American production would see to that. Roosevelt spelled out the plan in typically American large, casual round numbers: 45,000 tanks in 1942, 75,000 in '43; 45,000 planes in 1942, 100,000 in '43; 8 million tons of merchant shipping in '42, 10 million in '43. Since a twentieth of that would have beaten Hitler in 1940, it seemed adequate; nobody thought the war could last longer than two years.

To make sure that good old American production was run with good old American efficiency, the press called, in somewhat un-American metaphor, for a "czar." Candidates blossomed at once: V.P. Henry Wallace, Secretary Morgenthau, and pushiest of the bunch, Bernard Baruch, who liked to pretend he preferred the background, but who actually longed for the foreground. Roosevelt wisely passed up all the volunteers in favor of Donald M. Nelson, a nice-guy, ex-Sears executive who had done an outstanding job already in defense production.

In Washington and in the country the mood was jubilant. The cause was so just that the budget didn't need to be balanced, and that took an awfully just cause. The blackout curtains in the White House, the new War Room (T.R.'s old Trophy Room) with its maps and pins and secrecy (because even Secret Service men were barred, the Navy officers who manned the War Room put in a course of wheelchair practice to handle the Commander in Chief's visits) were all exciting, even fun. Trips to Hyde Park were made under cover of a loose security, beneath which bubbled happy togetherness for the Boss and staff. Instead of boarding the Ferdinand Magellan (who picked that name for the Presidential train?) at the usual platform under the Bureau of Engraving Annex, the party slipped off to some inconspicuous station like Silver Spring, Maryland, where a mystified station master was holding a special train. Cocktails and sandwiches aboard, then to bed, arriving early in the morning at Highland, New York. On the first trip Steve Early's assistant, Bill Hassett, checked in with the Poughkeepsie papers to make sure they printed nothing about the eight square-shouldered men who registered at the Campbell House hotel, but on later trips the Secret Service was put up at the Vanderbilt estate, just north of Hyde Park.

176

That Roosevelt grin, 1942

Hassett began the day by bringing the mail pouch up to Roosevelt's bedroom. If the President was in the bathroom shaving, he cheerily invited Hassett to "have a seat on the can." Sometimes the routine varied; one morning Roosevelt was off in the woods before dawn, identifying bird calls; another time, when Harry Hopkins brought Paulette Goddard up from New York for lunch, Roosevelt got the day started promptly by driving over to the Vanderbilt house in his hand-operated Ford, reading and signing the mail on the spot.

For weekends when the pressure did not admit a long trip to Hyde Park, the group made a short one to Shangri-La. This was a former

Brig. Gen. James Doolittle received the Congressional Medal of Honor after his spectacular raid on Tokyo on April 18, 1942.

CCC camp in the Catoctin Hills of Maryland, sixty-five miles from Washington, which had been converted into a small hunting lodge. It consisted of a main house with four bedrooms and two baths, and a scatter of tiny cottages. The Secret Service found it perfect—it was surrounded by a Marine training camp and was hard to spot from the air. The accommodations were a little sporting—among other things, Sherwood found that the guest bathroom wouldn't lock. The master bath was done over with a higher bowl and basin, and lower mirror, and outside Roosevelt's bedroom a drawbridge-like trapdoor was cut into the wall as a fire escape. Shangri-La did have one advantage over the White House—the cooking was done by the Filipino crew of the drydocked *Potomac*.

178

But all was euphoric in 1942; at Shangri-La, Hyde Park, and Pennsylvania Avenue, Roosevelt felt great. With a sure instinct which he shared with the public, he was undismayed by the headlined Japanese victories in the Pacific. Eventually, as he promised in the Pearl Harbor speech, the Japs were going to get theirs.

Neither Roosevelt nor the Japanese had an inkling that the memo from the S-1 section of the Office of Scientific Research and Development that he had airily approved—"O.K.—F.D.R." was a death warrant for a pair of obscure Japanese cities some years hence. Roosevelt approved the huge outlays for the Manhattan Project because it was easy and because the scientists told him, through the layers of committees, that the Germans were working on an A-bomb. How little he thought of it is demonstrated by his failure ever to mention it to Harry Truman.

In that spring of 1942 the Japanese offensive wilted in the Pacific. Early in June, alerted by another intercepted broken-code message, the Navy recouped Pearl Harbor with a sensational win at Midway. One of the heroes of the fight was the PWA's *Yorktown,* which met a glorious death after a lion's share in the victory.

A few days later Winston Churchill made the Washington scene. He had paid a trumpeted visit just after Pearl Harbor, when the United Nations was proclaimed (not as a world organization, just as a name for the Allies). At that time the press read his purpose as seeking to hold Roosevelt to a "Germany first" war policy, but the truth was more like the opposite. Churchill wanted Japan stopped from moving in on his Empire. "Our first Imperial obligation was to defend India from the Japanese," he still maintained in his memoirs. "To leave four hundred million of His Majesty's subjects, to whom we were bound in honour, to be ravaged and overrun . . . would have been a deed of shame. . . . Our Indian Empire, with all its glories, might fall an easy prey. . . ." Roosevelt had the temerity to suggest that one approach to the defense of India might be to conciliate the Indian independence movement, which Japan sought to exploit. Churchill blew sky-high. How could the Indian Empire with all its glories be preserved by giving the Indians their independence? Instead he threw Gandhi and Nehru in jail, never mind the Atlantic Charter. In Parliament he blamed the fall of Singapore on America's shield being "dashed to the ground" at Pearl Harbor. That made the U.S. Navy steam, but old pro Roosevelt shrugged it off: "Winston had to say *something.*"

Probably the most significant thing about the Churchill visit in December '41 was the subtle shift in status that emerged. The Chinese Foreign Minister underlined it—to Churchill's vexation he hailed

179

FRANKLIN D. ROOSEVELT

Roosevelt as "Commander-in-chief of the United Nations." Not only did Roosevelt politely lecture Churchill on the sins of Empire, but he overruled him on military matters. Churchill sought to establish British primacy in war leadership, both for the honor of the thing and to steer American power toward a defense of British imperial interests. He had the extraordinary nerve to propose that the B-17s and B-24s sent to Britain should be flown exclusively by the RAF, and that the Foreign Office should take charge of Lend-Lease distribution to European and Mediterranean countries. Roosevelt turned down the Lend-Lease proposal, and stoutly backed his own air generals on an American air force in Britain.

Franklin was fascinated by royalty, especially Queen Wilhelmina of The Netherlands.

During a trip to inspect war plants, Roosevelt visited Mrs. Elliott Roosevelt and family in Fort Worth.

But the most important argument with Churchill came over the invasion of Western Europe. This was the key strategic question of the war. Marshall and Eisenhower (chief of the War Plans Division) drew up a memorandum for Roosevelt giving all the reasons why this operation had to get top priority. They wanted to seize a bridgehead in Normandy, hopefully in the autumn of 1942, to use as a base for a win-the-war offensive in the spring and summer of '43.

Churchill did not favor the Marshall-Eisenhower strategy one bit. Timid and wary behind his cigar-chewing bluster, Churchill wanted to fight Germany from a safe distance by dropping bombs on German cities after dark. This strategy had its theoretical basis in the fanciful writings of Italian General Douhet. Bomb the enemy's cities, said Douhet, and the enemy will come running out with hands up. Marshall, while valuing air power, was convinced that the GIs were going to have to walk into Germany firing their M-1s.

181

Many problems involving Lend-Lease were brought to the President's attention by its administrator, Edward Stettinius, Jr.

To prevent the Normandy landing (variously coded as SLEDGE-HAMMER and ROUNDUP, and eventually as OVERLORD) was Churchill's purpose in his June 1942 visit. In Washington and at Hyde Park he was at his most orotund in warning Roosevelt of the peril: "The Channel will be a river of blood," he tirelessly declaimed. Stimson and Hopkins urged Roosevelt to hold firm behind Marshall and Eisenhower, and it looked as if Churchill would be overruled again. Churchill pinned some hopes on a victory his generals were planning in Africa which might shine up British prestige enough to make Roosevelt listen to him. But something went wrong in Africa and instead of a victory the British took a bad defeat.

A neutral observer might figure that the combination of tremendous American victory at Midway and unaccountable British defeat in Africa (after all, the whole German army was tied up in Russia)

With Eleanor Roosevelt on the porch of the Executive Office in 1942.

would have brought an American take-over of the strategy department. Strangely enough, the very opposite happened. General Auchinleck's blunders did what Churchill's eloquence probably could not have done—they canceled the invasion of Western Europe for 1942, and by a fatal chain reaction, for 1943.

It was a Sunday morning (June 21, 1942), back in the White

House after a visit to Hyde Park, when Roosevelt handed Churchill a message from the War Room reporting the fall of Tobruk (Libya). With it went not a word of criticism, then or later—only commiseration. In his memoirs Churchill could not suppress a note of astonishment at the "delicacy and kindness" of his ally. Though Marshall and Hopkins at first continued to fight for SLEDGEHAMMER-ROUNDUP, the British retreat into Egypt shoved it to the back of the planning stove. Messages went out re-scheduling shipments, even re-routing ships at sea. Hundreds of Sherman tanks designated for the invasion of Normandy were re-directed around the Cape of Good Hope. When Roosevelt agreed to order forty Douglas A-20s already entering the Persian Gulf, en route to the Russian front, re-routed to Egypt, even Churchill was a little worried. But Stalin, reached by cable, surprisingly gave his O.K. He had no inkling that he was contributing to the postponement of the Second Front on which he heavily counted, or that the Murmansk convoys, just beginning to give him some help, were about to be suspended owing to heavy losses. Chiang Kai-shek, on the other hand, told that some of his airplanes were going to Egypt, screamed his head off, but even though Mme. Chiang threatened to make a separate peace with Japan, nobody paid any attention.

It was 14,000 miles from port of New York to Egypt via the Cape of Good Hope, which equaled four times across the Atlantic to Normandy. But logic and logistics notwithstanding, everything shippable went pell-mell to Egypt. Admiral King, seeing the Normandy invasion thrown out, said how about starting something in the Pacific? Marshall, disgusted with Churchill, gave King support. Roosevelt could scarcely refuse. He approved a plan for an offensive against Japan in the ugly, jungly Solomon Islands, which turned out to be a rotten place to fight. So did every other island the Marines and Army hit in the next three long years. Roosevelt's original intention, to hold tight in the Pacific, finish off Hitler, and then confront Japan, would have been far wiser. The Pacific GIs won every battle, but there wasn't a laugher in the series.

Worse yet was the effect of the June decisions on the war against Germany. Something had to be done to satisfy the public outcry in Britain and the United States for a Second Front (not to mention the private outcry from Stalin). The answer was found in a plan called Operation TORCH, a landing in, of all places, French North Africa. TORCH appealed to Churchill because it was so safe. He tried to sell it to Marshall by knocking the quality of American soldiers, saying those rookies just were not ready for Hitler's varsity. Marshall didn't buy that, but he could hardly prevent TORCH. So in the fall, with Germans and Russians locked in the decisive battle of our era at Stalingrad, the best that powerful America could contribute was a landing in irrelevant, immaterial French North Africa (November 7–8, 1942).

If some of the long-range consequences were tragic, some of the short-range ones were comic. Cordell Hull had taken a mysterious but terrific dislike to De Gaulle, which he transmitted in some degree to Roosevelt. A scheme was cooked up by Hull's none-too-bright young men in the State Department to keep De Gaulle out of North Africa, and afterwards out of France, by giving Eisenhower another French general, somebody no one had ever heard of, named Giraud. General Giraud went on the radio to order French troops in North Africa to stop firing on the Allies, but they paid no attention, so Eisenhower had to make a deal with Pétain's man, Admiral Darlan. That brought flak from the press and embarrassment for Roosevelt

Maj. James Roosevelt helped capture a Japanese battle flag, but F.D.R. wanted no part of it when it was presented to him by Lt. Gen. Thomas Holcomb of the Marines.

It was "Rosie the Riveter" in gabardine overalls and a hairnet who manned the defense plants visited by the President on his September 1942 inspection trip.

and Eisenhower. Somebody (could it have been the OSS?) solved the problem by having Darlan assassinated. But no matter how Hull and his assistants reassured Roosevelt that the French loved Giraud and couldn't stand De Gaulle (who among other things was supposed to be "in Churchill's pocket") it was fairly evident that something was wrong—in Algiers, De Gaulle's flag got all the cheers. Churchill and Eden, mystified by the American attitude, suggested a combined Giraud–De Gaulle government, and Roosevelt decided to call an on-the-spot (or near-the-spot) conference.

Just before leaving for Casablanca he received a delegation at the White House headed by Rabbi Stephen Wise of New York. Rabbi Wise's connection with Roosevelt dated back to 1931, when he and other liberals had pressed the governor hard on the Jimmy Walker case. The resulting slight tiff paved the way to a lifelong friendship. In their correspondence Wise always addressed Roosevelt as "Dear Boss," and their meetings usually involved a few laughs. But this time Wise was not in a laughing mood. He presented Roosevelt with a document entitled, "Blueprint for Extermination," which was a country-by-country report on the plans and progress of Hitler's

186

Final Solution. Based on Swiss sources with connections inside the Nazi government, the paper made the massive scale and grisly reality of the extermination program, about which some rumors had appeared in the press, fully credible. Expressing profound shock, Roosevelt assured the delegation that every step would be taken to end the crimes, to identify the criminals for later trial, and to "save those who can yet be saved."

There was a long, dismal history behind Rabbi Wise's visit. The State Department had met every appeal on behalf of the threatened Jews of Europe with a tactic of silence and delay. The nearest approach the U.S. government ever made to saving anybody was a courageous fight back in 1939 by Senator Wagner and Eleanor Roosevelt to get 20,000 refugee children admitted. All the patriotic organizations in the country—the veterans, the DAR, Sara Roosevelt's Society of Mayflower Descendants—rose in defense, not of the Constitution or the Bill of Rights, but of the 1922 immigration quotas. (The next year when somebody suggested admitting several thousand English children outside the quota, the bill slid through like greased lightning.)

"Well, God bless you, sir. I'm glad to see you," former Vice-President Garner shouted to F.D.R. when they met on the Presidential train in Uvalde, Texas, September 1942.

Casablanca Conference, January 1943. On its final day, F.D.R. and Churchill met the press. The rival French generals, Henri Giraud and Charles de Gaulle forced a handshake for photographers.

Unfortunately, by late 1942 there was no way, in the light of Hitler's satanic determination, to save the three million East European Jews (or the 200,000 Gypsies, for whom Hitler also had no use, and large numbers of other people) except by a swift Allied victory. Operation TORCH almost ruled that out, and the Casablanca Conference completed the job.

After a train trip to Miami, the Presidential party boarded a Boeing clipper (flying boat), refueling in Belém, Brazil, before taking off on an 18½-hour flight across the waist of the South Atlantic to Bathurst, an old slave-trade station converted to an air-ferry base. A C-54 took them on to Casablanca, where Churchill waited, effulgent with the victory at El Alamein which all those turned-around and re-routed Sherman tanks had bought. He promptly laid down the "task" facing the conference: ". . . to conquer the African shores of the Mediterranean . . . and . . . to strike at the underbelly of the Axis," which he identified as Sicily, Crete, Rhodes —anything but France. Marshall argued hard, but he was outflanked. To keep TORCH completely free of risk, the Tunisian ports had been omitted from the landings. Hitler had promptly grabbed them, so the Allies were faced with a six-month fight in Tunisia.

188

After that it would be too late to organize SLEDGEHAMMER for spring, and Churchill already had all kinds of reasons for invading Sicily and southern Italy. Thus a minor British defeat in a sideshow theater virtually determined the course of the war, and sealed the fate of millions.

The conference (January 1943) also had a political side, the continuation of the De Gaulle–Giraud comic opera. De Gaulle proved a tough, smart competitor who, though outnumbered and bullied, successfully fought off the attempt to use him as window dressing in a Giraud military dictatorship. Roosevelt, beginning to sense the State Department's blundering, fell back on heavy-handed humor about a shotgun wedding and a Joan of Arc complex.

The biggest news story to come out of Casablanca (apart from the startler that a President had flown the Atlantic, and in fact had flown at all—even that was a first) was Roosevelt's "unconditional surrender" toss-off. Much ink was spent pointing out that this was grist for Goebbels. Maybe, but it hardly helped the Nazis as much as the decision to postpone SLEDGEHAMMER.

Despite Churchill's getting his way on strategy, Casablanca marked a further shift in the inter-Allied relationship toward Roosevelt. America was now putting out all those tanks, planes, jeeps, weapons carriers, 50-caliber MGs, C-rations, sound-power telephones, and the rest. On top of all that the GIs were in combat, and proving they could fight Germans and beat them, Churchill to the contrary notwithstanding.

Roosevelt was now senior partner. The change was dramatized by a dinner Roosevelt gave for the Sultan of Morocco. Churchill squirmed while the Sultan listened enraptured to the American President's exposition of how old-fashioned imperialist exploitation must cease and the underdeveloped countries be helped. Who would do the helping? American business firms, Roosevelt declared, without finding anything funny about it.

Did Lord Acton smile somewhere? Maybe, but Roosevelt had the advantage as well as the drawback of American innocence. He believed American influence would create a better world, and his belief gave American influence at least a slight push in the direction of trying to create one.

11

"Victory and Peace"

IN 1943 the pins in the War Room moved too slowly. Salerno, Anzio, Cassino—the American-British-French-Polish Allied army found the road to Rome a hard way to go. In the wide spaces of the Pacific the Marines advanced one bloody pin after another. The convoys to Murmansk, also plotted on the map, ran into hell, too. From his wheelchair Roosevelt, who knew all the cargoes, sometimes shook his head and said, "There go [X number] of P-38s we can't afford to lose."

The air war knocked down buildings and buried people, but did not make a prophet out of Douhet. Despite extravagant expenditures, esoteric target study, and hard-nosed determination—fifty-four B-17s and 24s, carrying 532 U.S. airmen, lost in one raid—German war production didn't shut down. On the contrary, it improved amazingly all through 1943 and right on into 1944.

Meantime the sealed boxcars kept rolling from eastern Europe, the Netherlands, and Belgium (though not from France or Italy, where Laval, Pétain, and Mussolini refused to go along with the Final Solution). Late in 1943 Henry Morgenthau, a conscientious if bumbling man, was aroused by the cold-blooded negativism of the State Department and the Foreign Office. Out of Morgenthau's representations came Roosevelt's creation of a War Refugee Board which tardily saved several thousand people and a piece of America's honor.

But Allied victory, the solitary hope of most of Hitler's victims, remained a postponed event. Churchill's blockade of SLEDGEHAMMER now threatened OVERLORD, the code designation of the cross-Channel assault in 1944. Roosevelt became convinced that a conference in-

F.D.R. and Winston try fishing at Shangri-La, one of the President's favorite weekend retreats.

cluding Stalin was indispensable. The capital of Iran, Teheran, was finally picked as a mutually suitable site, and a tie-in meeting arranged with Chiang Kai-shek at Cairo. The complicated double conference was scheduled for late November 1943.

The big new battleship *Iowa,* one of the last clutch of instant antiques laid down by the Navy, was pre-empted for the trip. By now the drill for these things was smooth. The inconspicuously loaded baggage included items from the checklist of Lieutenant Rigdon, assistant to the Naval Aide:

Money (Roosevelt never carried a cent)

Special foods (Not for Roosevelt, but for others, like Pa Watson, lovable old military aide, who liked hominy grits)

Booze, plus Saratoga Springs water for Roosevelt

192

Kitchen matches (for safe smoking in bed)

Deep-sea fishing gear

Playing cards and poker chips (again, not for Roosevelt)

Reading matter, including guides to countries to be visited, and mystery novels for both Roosevelt's and Hopkins' bedtimes.

Films—enough for a movie every night aboard.

Discussions over fishing lines and cocktail glasses centered on the upcoming strategic decision—Operation OVERLORD (ex-ROUNDUP). The problem was how to make Churchill swallow it. Stimson, in his parting message, had stated fervently: "The one prayer I make for the Commander-in-Chief is steadfastness." Hopkins, once Churchill's cheerleader, agreed that the time had come to "line up with the Russians . . . There's just no god-damn alternative left."

In Cairo little was accomplished beyond a Thanksgiving dinner at which Roosevelt carved American turkeys while he and Churchill competed in cornball requests to the GI orchestra—"Carry Me Back to Ol' Virginny" and "Ol' Man River" by the P.M., and something called "The White Cliffs of Dover" by the President. A projected campaign in Burma was discussed with Chiang, but Roosevelt hardly got any farther with the Chinese generalissimo and his steely-eyed wife than had General Stilwell, Chiang's American ad-

Churchill, Roosevelt and the Chiang Kai-sheks at the Cairo Conference.

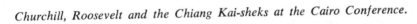

En route home, the President touched down in Sicily to review troops with Gen. Eisenhower on December 8, 1943.

viser. Basically the trouble was that the Americans wanted the Chinese army to do some fighting, a proposal Chiang found distasteful. So notorious was Chinese uncombativeness among U.S. military men that the Chiangs were suspected of being secretly pro-Japanese; when Mme. Chiang visited the White House and Eleanor innocently took her to the War Room, the Navy officers jumped to switch the pins around, convinced that any ship location the Chiangs found out about would soon be known in Tokyo.

There are no records of exactly what was said at the Cairo conference—Mme. Chiang did the translating and nobody took any notes. Churchill skips over it lightly in his memoirs; he himself had no enthusiasm for the Burma plan because, Burma being part of the Empire, he didn't want it liberated by a lot of Chinese.

The 1300-mile journey from Cairo to Teheran was made by air, in the C-54 which somebody nicknamed the "Sacred Cow." Ross McIntire worried about flying over mountains—Roosevelt had long had a sinus problem which was now getting worse—but they made it without trouble. The original intention was for the Presidential party to put up at the American Embassy, but Stalin, who assumed responsibility for security arrangements, expressed concern over the distance Roosevelt had to drive each day in a city known to be infested with enemy agents. At the suggestion of the Russian dictator, Roosevelt moved into a villa inside the Russian Embassy compound, where NKVD agents made the Presidential bed, pistols bulging under their white tunics.

Fifteen minutes after Roosevelt's arrival Stalin called. Stocky, graying, wearing his new marshal's uniform, he made clear at once his respect for the American leader who had saved capitalism. Well aware that Roosevelt alone was capable of overruling Churchill on OVERLORD, he was gratified to learn that this was Roosevelt's intention. In the meetings that followed, Churchill sought in his usual slippery fashion to approve OVERLORD in theory but avoid it in reality by earmarking troops and landing craft for minor Mediterranean operations. He argued eloquently for an effort to bring Turkey into the war, but Roosevelt pointed out that the necessary bribe in planes, tanks, and other arms would kill OVERLORD. Outnumbered, and sensing Roosevelt's determination, Churchill executed a strategic retreat, and allowed a target date to be set for OVERLORD: May 1, 1944. To nail the plan down Stalin asked Roosevelt to name the commander. The choice lay between Marshall and Eisenhower; though Stalin would have accepted Ulysses S. Grant if it brought

On inspection, the President receives a model bomber from workers at the Douglas Aircraft Company in Tulsa, April 19, 1943.

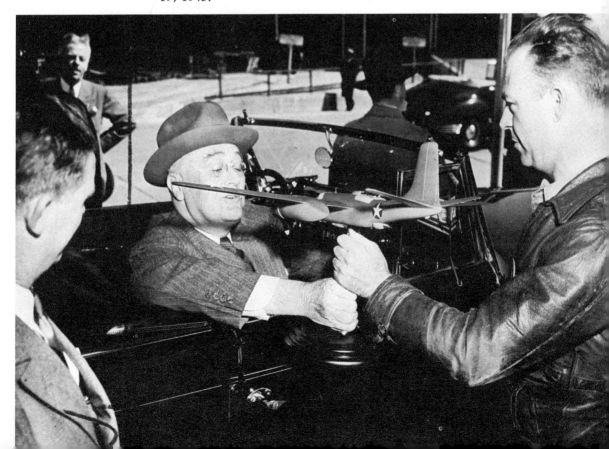

A New York taxicab with a radio draws a large crowd to listen to a Presidential address.

OVERLORD any closer, he favored Marshall as the man who showed the most determined interest. In the end Roosevelt picked Eisenhower over the strenuous objections of Stimson and the silent but bitter disappointment of Marshall, simply because, as he told Marshall, "I could not sleep at night with you out of the country."

Apart from the OVERLORD decision, the Teheran conference did little except give official stamp to decisions already taken—Stalin to enter the Pacific war in return for recovery of the Czar's 1905 losses; Russia to get the Curzon Line in Poland and Poland to get Silesia. Stalin was more cordial toward Roosevelt's scheme to turn the UN into a world organization than he had been before, on condition that he get a veto in the Security Council. That paved the way for the Dumbarton Oaks discussions the following August, and the eventual San Francisco charter meetings. One serious cloud appeared—Stalin gave fairly blunt notice of his intentions in regard to the government of Poland, and by implication toward those of the other East European countries.

196

On the cocktail level, Teheran went fine, with no more embarrassments than at most parties. The one everybody remembered afterward (though from Elliott Roosevelt to Lord Moran everybody remembered it differently) was when Stalin proposed a toast to shooting 50,000 Nazis after the war. That made Churchill splutter—he thought (according to Moran) that any number of Germans could be killed in hot blood, like dropping bombs on them, but only a few in cold. Seeing Churchill so purple, Roosevelt kidded the thing, and Stalin joined in. Nobody mentioned the Final Solution.

Roosevelt caught a bad cold and old Pa Watson had a stroke. Ross McIntire forbade either of them to fly at over 8000 feet, so the last day of the conference was rushed through to beat the weather. Back in the United States, Roosevelt needed a rest. He wanted to go to Guantanamo, but the Secret Service said no. Bernard Baruch offered his South Carolina estate, where convalescence was achieved with some irritation. Instead of politely clearing out

British foreign secretary Anthony Eden greeted the President in Quebec for a conference on the invasion of Europe.

U.P.I.

*General Dwight Eisenhower received the Legion of Merit
from the President at the Cairo Conference, November 1943.*

and leaving the place to Roosevelt, Baruch hung ostentatiously
around. On top of that, the fish wouldn't bite and McIntire cut the
liquor ration to one drink a day. Finally the patient turned the corner, McIntire took the lid off, and one afternoon in the boat Roosevelt exclaimed, "My God, I've caught a fish!"

There was no question that physically he was slipping. Long kept
from normal exercise, his body had aged beyond his chronological
sixty-two years. McIntire put him on a diet and he began to acquire
a slack, scrawny-neck look. Sherwood, after not seeing him for
several months, noticed the difference with dismay. Yet with OVER-
LORD not even launched, Roosevelt's hope (originally a conviction)
that he was headed for the Florida fishing lodge in a year was
doomed. Mere deterioration could not excuse him from running; there
was no such speculation in '44 as had filled the air in '40. It was
taken for granted that a Commander in Chief did not quit during a
war.

He tried to conserve his energy. When Churchill proposed to come
over again with some new reasons for postponing OVERLORD, Roose-

velt gave him a firm turndown. Churchill's gusty charm was wearing thin anyway. Changing his tack, the P.M. sought to get the invasion army put under British command. He proposed that Eisenhower sit at the top as a sort of honorary chairman of the board, while the air, naval, and ground forces each be headed by a British commander in chief. The American military were willing to give in on naval and air, but since the ground force was overwhelmingly GI, why should little Montgomery, who wasn't exactly an American favorite anyway, run the show? Roosevelt backed Marshall in resisting, but perhaps he might have backed him a push farther, because the upshot was an unsatisfactory compromise that may have delayed victory. Montgomery was given command of all the ground forces until the breakout from Normandy, then he had to divide up with Omar Bradley. When the breakout came, the whole German army was almost, but not quite, trapped; at least one reason the Falaise gap wasn't closed was that Brad and Monty didn't communicate.

While the battle raged in Normandy, the Republicans and Democrats held their nominating conventions. Interest among the Democrats centered on the Vice-Presidency. The bosses were after Roosevelt to dump Henry Wallace. Hopeful replacements volunteered all around. Roosevelt leaned toward Justice Douglas, while National Chairman Bob Hannegan pushed fellow-Missourian Harry Truman. Once more Chicago was the scene of feverish maneuvering. Hannegan scored a coup when Roosevelt's train, en route to the West Coast for the beginning of an inspection trip that would take him to Alaska and the Aleutians, stopped incognito in Chicago. Sneaking on board, Hannegan got Roosevelt to have Grace Tully retype a note in which the Presidential benediction had been bestowed on Douglas and Truman. In the retyped version, Truman's name came first. Armed with that, Hannegan quickly put Truman over, except for one detail—Truman himself, taken completely by surprise, came close to declining. At the last minute Hannegan got Roosevelt on the phone in San Diego and Truman, sitting on the bed in Hannegan's room at the Blackstone, listened incredulously as Roosevelt's hearty voice came in: "Bob, have you got that fellow lined up yet?"

The Republicans put up young Tom Dewey to contrast with the tired, crippled old man in the White House. Dewey hammered away at the health issue, but not really with conviction; Dewey no more than anyone else knew how tired and sick Roosevelt was. On the West Coast trip he had a seizure, apparently a heart attack; only Jimmy Roosevelt, whose Fifth Marine Division the President had come to inspect, was with him in his railroad car. Assisting him to stretch out flat on the car floor, Jimmy waited helplessly

199

Eleanor and Franklin at Hyde Park, 1943

till the attack passed. "Get me up, now, Jimmy," the stricken man said, and went out to the review. A bad speech in Bremerton, Washington, where he had trouble simultaneously holding himself erect and turning the pages, started a few rumors. That may have roused his fighting spirit. Summoning reserves from somewhere, he surprised and delighted the entourage with a resurgence of vitality. Once again there was the lively, bantering oral speech-writing while the President mixed cocktails, followed by buffet, in the Oval Room with Hopkins, Rosenman, and Sherwood throwing in ideas, objecting, revising, and Roosevelt dictating to Grace Tully, sometimes rambling to an untidy halt: "Something along those lines—you boys fix it up." He threw in personal insults at the opposition just for the hell of it, knowing they would be taken out. The first draft was always far too long. Turning at once to the last page he announced cheerfully, "Ninety-two per cent has to be cut." Then he would think of an insert, and start out, "Grace, take a law. Insert A, page three . . ."

200

*In Oceanside, California, to observe an amphibious
landing maneuver, July 20, 1944*

When he wheeled off to bed, Sherwood and Rosenman stayed
up and reworked. Sometimes Eleanor, a late worker herself, came
around at three A.M. and told them it was bedtime.

While Dewey stumped the country, Roosevelt stuck to the East
Coast on the excuse that the Commander in Chief could not stray
far from Washington. But he had that radio. Addressing the Teamsters Union, he set the nation laughing and maybe won the fight
with one punch. Somebody—Republican headquarters was suspect
—had set a rumor going that he had ordered a destroyer, at heavy
cost to the taxpayers, to go back to Alaska to pick up his Scottie,
Fala, accidentally left behind.

"The Republican leaders," Roosevelt told the truck drivers and
the radio audience, "have not been content to make personal attacks
upon me, or my wife, or my sons. [Boos] They now include my

The President conferred with some of his top military officers in Hawaii in July 1944. From left: Gen. Douglas MacArthur, F.D.R., Adm. Chester Nimitz, and Adm. William Leahy. Below, Adm. Nimitz reviews strategy with Gen. MacArthur, the President, and Adm. Leahy.

Discussing campaign strategy and getting acquainted are the President and his 1944 running mate, Harry Truman.

little dog Fala. [Laughter] Unlike the members of my family, Fala resents this. [Guffaws] When he learned that the Republican fiction writers had concocted a story that I had left him behind on an Aleutian island and had sent a destroyer back to find him, at a cost to the taxpayer of two or three or twenty million dollars, his Scotch soul was furious . . . [Roars]."

Dewey, whose trouble was that he came across a little chilly, had his picture taken with his big white Pyrenees shepherd. Tart Harold Ickes creamed him: "This is a contest between a little man with a big dog and a big man with a little dog."

The campaign climaxed with a motorcade in New York. By terrible luck it poured rain all day long. Roosevelt went right through with the schedule, in open car, soaked to the skin, stopping midway in a Brooklyn garage to make a complete change of clothes. The New York crowds, who knew a champ when they saw one, jammed the streets. Before going to a stuffy dinner he changed

A tired President, looking older than his 62 years, arrived in New York City for a speaking engagement at Hunter College, October 22, 1944.

clothes again at the Washington Square apartment Eleanor had rented in anticipation of a '44 retirement.

They listened to the returns at Hyde Park as usual, with the crowd from the village gathering by torchlight to applaud his cheery victory speech. The plurality was down from '40, but it was clear early in the evening that he had won, with the soldier vote providing a sizable piece of the margin. Understandably, he was gratified, but his characterization of the campaign as "the dirtiest in all history" was a gross exaggeration. His opinion of Dewey, expressed as he wheeled in to bed, as "that son of a bitch," was scarcely warranted. It wasn't really Dewey, or Dewey's charges that he was old and sick, that bugged him. It was the fact that he *was* old and sick, that he felt down more of the time and up less of it.

He went off to Warm Springs for a Thanksgiving rest before going back to work in Washington, then Christmas in Hyde Park with the grandchildren around the fire. He shortened his annual reading of "A Christmas Carol," which usually took him three nights. In January (1945) he returned to Washington for his fourth inauguration. The family was struck afterwards by the recollection that he had gone to great lengths—putting in long-distance calls, paying railroad fares—to make sure that every one of the thirteen grandchildren was there. He also spent some time digging out mementos for the children and grandchildren.

The Secret Service recommended that the ceremony be held at the White House instead of the Capitol, and Roosevelt readily acquiesced. Taking the oath on the South Portico from Chief Justice Harlan Stone (the surviving liberal of the Nine Old Men had gotten his reward), Roosevelt looked and sounded strong—"ready for anything the next four years might bring," Sherwood thought. He wasn't, though. Just before lunch, to which an enormous crowd was invited, he retreated to the Green Room with Jimmy, home on leave. Though he had kept his address down to five minutes, he was chilled. "Jimmy," he said. "I can't take this unless you get me a stiff drink."

Two days later he was aboard the cruiser *Quincy,* en route to Yalta. Another conference with Churchill, and especially with Stalin, seemed essential for nailing down arrangements made by the foreign ministers on occupation of Germany. Eleanor wanted to go along to make sure he took care of himself, but her presence seemed inappropriate—it wasn't the sort of thing you brought wives to. Instead he took Anna.

Stalin, who didn't fly (either too scared or too sensible), had insisted on Yalta because he didn't want to be more than an

205

Always a vigorous campaigner, the President, with Eleanor beside him, rides through New York City's garment district. At left, he speaks to an enthusiastic audience in Poughkeepsie during the 1944 campaign.

old-fashioned sleeper jump from Moscow. The *Quincy* first landed the Presidential party at Malta for a rendezvous with Churchill and his suite. The latest British scheme was unveiled—Eisenhower should give Monty enough U.S. troops and supplies to enable him to go capture Berlin ahead of the Russians—never mind the agreement already made on zones. Eisenhower resisted on tactical grounds (besides, why should that so-and-so Montgomery grab all the glory?)

and Marshall peremptorily announced that if Roosevelt approved Churchill's plan he would recommend to Ike that he resign his command. In a heated showdown, Roosevelt stuck solidly behind his generals, adding one more to the list of things for which Churchill never forgave him.

Before the C-54s took off for Yalta, Secret Service Chief Mike Reilly arranged for GI sergeants to be attached to Russian AA batteries in the flight path to avoid an unhappy accident. The Presidential party found the eighty-mile road from the airport more of a hazard than the flight. The roads were rough, the curves sharp, the precipices steep, the retaining walls non-existent, and the Russian drivers nonchalant. The scene was lined with Russian soldiers ("Look how many of them are girls!" Anna exclaimed) and littered with wrecked tanks, overturned railroad cars, and burned-out buildings.

Roosevelt occupied the Czar's ground-floor apartment in Livadia Palace, but the Germans had stripped the place clean, and the Russians had shipped furnishings down from a not-very-luxurious Moscow hotel. The scarcity of bathrooms was aggravated by Stalinist security—generals and admirals stepping out on the grass before bedtime were shoved back into the palace to wait their turn.

Few of the problems on the Yalta agenda were troublesome. Zone boundaries for the occupation of Germany were already laid down by the foreign ministers; now pushy De Gaulle (whose wild reception in Paris had caused Roosevelt to re-evaluate those State

Driving around Hyde Park with Fala, October 1944

U.P.I.

The last family portrait at the White House, January 20, 1945

Department briefings) wanted an occupation zone. Churchill, tardily waking up to the fact that the Red Army was about to camp on the Elbe with nothing between it and the Channel except the Americans, who said they weren't staying, backed De Gaulle, whose new French First Army was already on the Rhine. Cordell Hull had resigned for reasons of ill health (though he lived ten more years). Roosevelt wisely and generously agreed to create a French zone out of the projected U.S. zone.

Stalin named a round number for German reparations: $20 billion, which did not stagger Roosevelt (Lend-Lease was adding up to $50 billion) though Churchill found it a bit steep. On the Pacific war, Stalin simply repeated his commitment and his price.

Poland alone created open friction. Churchill argued vehemently for the Polish government in London, and Roosevelt supported him eloquently, but it was no go. Stalin's intransigence was rooted too deeply. The best Roosevelt could get was a promise to let a few of the London Poles join a Russian-picked Warsaw government.

What really made Yalta so different from Teheran was not the diplomatic decisions—almost nothing was added to or subtracted from those already made—but the change in the military picture.

208

With Hitler on the verge of defeat, and the Red Army battling in the streets of Budapest, the problem of the power vacuum in Europe became more real, and more contentious. An earlier OVERLORD might have brought the end with the Russian army still in Russia, for all Germans, Nazi or not, infinitely preferred the Americans to the Russians. Stalin himself pointed out that the Germans gave up large cities in the heart of Germany to the Americans, while fighting the Russians for obscure towns "which they need as much as a dead man needs a poultice."

The military convergence of the Allies made Yalta a tense session. Stalin and Churchill, no longer hiding their antagonism with flattery, snarled openly. Though still the dominant member of the Big Three, Roosevelt did not command the respect he had at Teheran. Nobody needed Lend-Lease that much any more.

With everybody older and crankier, even Churchill's afternoon nap caused trouble. Not wanting to go all the way back to his own digs after lunch, the P.M. asked Hopkins if he could snooze at Livadia. Hopkins, who looked terrible and was actually in bad shape, wouldn't give up his own bed, where he spent most of his time, but offered the room of Pa Watson and Wilson Brown, the military aides. But those two old gentlemen also needed their naps, and only gave in when Hopkins threatened to call Roosevelt from *his* bed.

Roosevelt foolishly crowded a visit with three kings of Orient

Jubilant after his fourth-term victory, F.D.R. returned to Washington from Hyde Park with Vice-President-elect Harry Truman and incumbent Vice-President Henry Wallace.

It was a more solemn inauguration in 1945. The ceremony took place on the White House portico; the address was brief.

into his voyage home. Ibn Saud of Arabia told him the surviving European Jews should be settled in Europe instead of in Palestine. Roosevelt agreed—nobody grasped the intractability of *that* problem yet.

Still another meeting had been scheduled—with De Gaulle in Algiers, but thorny De Gaulle was sore about being left out of Yalta, and didn't show. That was just as well. The tired and sick old men Dewey had waged his campaign against were tireder and sicker than ever. Aboard the *Quincy* Pa Watson had another stroke and died, and Harry Hopkins had to drop out at Algiers and rest at Marrakech, from which he presently flew to the Mayo Clinic, too ill to stop in Washington. Roosevelt reached the White House exhausted, lonely, and depressed. In his report to Congress, what many newsmen and congressmen noted most was that for

210

President Roosevelt and Vice-President Truman during the White House Inauguration, January 20, 1945.

the first time in his public life he made a direct reference to his polio. He apologized for delivering his speech sitting down, owing to "about ten pounds of steel on my legs."

Eleanor was even more struck by an incident a few days later. For twenty-five years she had made the nation's and the world's problems the main subject at the dinner table, often, when the kids were home, producing raging arguments (Burt Wheeler, present at one such dinner, said even Congress was never that bad). But now suddenly Eleanor discovered that the man who had reveled in noisy debates was too weary for serious talk. "For the first time," she wrote pathetically, "he could not bear to have a real discussion, such as we had always had."

The pressures continued—Churchill's vehement cables about Stalin, Stalin's mercurial suspicions about German peace feelers, the simmering Cabinet rivalries, the Congressional complaints—until March 29, when Roosevelt was wheeled up the ramp to the Ferdinand Magellan, bound for R & R at Warm Springs.

Anna would have gone with him but was held in Washington

211

Churchill and Soviet Foreign Minister Molotov await the President at Saki Airport in the Crimea for the Yalta Conference, February 3, 1945.

The President was tired, though all parties looked rested and agreeable here as they posed at Yalta, February 9, 1945.

F.D.R. and Churchill arguing a point after dinner at Yalta.

Averell Harriman and Premier Stalin greet each other during the Yalta Conference.

by the sickness of her young son. Instead two lady cousins, Laura Delano and Margaret Suckley, went along to help supply the "touch of triviality." Eleanor was either too busy or not invited—she wrote afterward that she was glad at the time that he had taken Laura and Margaret instead of her, because "they would not bother him as I would discussing affairs of state." The affairs of state, in the form of bags of mail, cablegrams, Congressional bills, of course pursued him.

But the weather was lovely, and on Monday, April 9, he got behind the wheel of his Ford. Mike Reilly followed in his Secret Service car. In the past Roosevelt had often gotten kicks out of ducking into back roads and losing the Secret Service, but this time he drove at a sedate pace through the country lanes bordered with dogwood in bloom to a crossroads rendezvous. Waiting there was a Cadillac convertible with three passengers: a Russian lady painter, Madame Shoumatoff; a photographer, Nicholas Robbins; and Lucy Mercer Rutherfurd.

Lucy had been with him at the Thanksgiving visit. She owned a portrait of him done by Mme. Shoumatoff, and now wanted to have another done for her daughter. Robbins was along to take color shots so the painter could complete the portrait after preliminary sittings.

The shooting occupied much of Tuesday. On Wednesday Roosevelt went for a drive with Lucy (and the Secret Service). He stopped the Ford at one of his favorite spots and sat gazing for a long time at the distant horizon—"as if looking onward and onward to some world of victory and peace," Mike Reilly told Grace Tully later.

The next day before lunch the artist was doing preliminary sketches, while Roosevelt finished the mail pouch Bill Hassett had brought. The two lady cousins and Lucy were there. Freshly signed papers were spread over chairs, the couch, the floor. "Bill's waiting for his laundry to dry," the President explained. Everybody was looking forward to a barbecue the mayor of Warm Springs and the manager of the Foundation had organized for the afternoon. Roosevelt's favorite Brunswick stew was on the menu.

"We've got just fifteen minutes more," he told Mme. Shoumatoff, and lit a cigarette. Then his arm dropped to his side. "I have a terrific headache," he said unexpectedly, and the next moment he closed his eyes and sagged in his chair.

It was a massive cerebral hemorrhage; in three hours he was dead without recovering consciousness. That quickly, the long story was over.

214

12
F. D. R.

THE VISITOR to Hyde Park today drives up through the tree-lined carriageway to the library, where he can examine baby Franklin's christening robe, the kilts Sara made him wear till he was eight, the Groton report cards, his letter to Sara about his engagement, the copy of Tasso a Venetian gondolier gave Eleanor on the honeymoon, and the desk from the White House, its jovial litter untouched since 1945. Strolling on past the rose garden where two gravestones stand side by side, he can tour the old house guided by Eleanor's friendly voice on tape—Sara's private sitting room, the library where Roosevelt served cocktails to the King and Queen despite Sara's insistence that tea would be more appropriate ("My mother would have said the same thing," confided George VI), the silent dining room where he further elevated the standard of American informality by first-naming a Crown Princess: "Juliana, Bill has a message for you" (imagine Hoover doing that), upstairs to the guest bedroom where Winston Churchill, Harry Hopkins, Louis Howe, and other great men slept, Sara's bedroom where her baby was born, and finally Roosevelt's own room, where he break-fasted in bed looking out on the shining Hudson far below. Folded at the foot of the bed is his dressing gown; on a chair before the fireplace are Fala's blanket and leash. In the dressing room on the right stands the old wheelchair. The half-open closet door reveals the comfortably battered Stetson, and the cape.

His presence is there, more vivid, if less tangible, than his impact on our lives.

Franklin D. Roosevelt was a complex man who defies ready sum-

215

The funeral train headed slowly north, here passing through Greenville, South Carolina, on its twenty-three-hour journey from Warm Springs to Washington. April 13, 1945.

marization. He was a revolutionary. No Che, no Mao, but a revolutionary. "Traditional as the words may have been in which the New Deal expressed itself," says historian Carl Degler, "in actuality it was a revolutionary response to a revolutionary situation." The country has never been the same since. Government spending—beg pardon, the public sector—is established as a way of capitalist life. Government responsibility for farm income, social security for the elderly, unemployment assistance, bank-deposit security, and all the rest of the modern welfare-state apparatus has been not only permanently fixed, but fixed in a state of indefinite expansion.

He was a maker of the American Presidency. Historian Clinton Rossiter says, "Only Washington . . . and Jackson . . . did more to raise it to its present condition of strength, dignity and in-

Aboard the train, four servicemen
at attention formed an honor guard
for the flag-draped casket
of President Roosevelt.

A solemn trio: Former War Mobilization Director James Byrnes, President
Harry S Truman, and Secretary of Commerce Henry Wallace await the
arrival of President Roosevelt's body at Union Station for services in the
East Room of the White House.

Mourners, often weeping, gathered in large numbers for a glimpse of the funeral procession heading for the capital on April 14. The next day, as Roosevelt was buried in Hyde Park, traffic stopped and silence was observed in New York's Times Square.

The twin townhouses at 47 and 49 East 65th Street in Manhattan built and decorated by Franklin's mother, Mrs. James Roosevelt, in 1908

The Roosevelt home at Hyde Park, New York

Inside the Hyde Park house, where the rooms remain furnished as they were when the Roosevelts were at home. Above, the living room. Below, Franklin's bedroom.

F.D.R.'s personal matchbook.

dependence." He turned the office into "an instrument of twentieth-century government" and in doing so, he may have "saved the Presidency from paralysis and the Constitution from radical amendment."

He was an example of leadership to the whole world. In the middle of the Depression, John Maynard Keynes wrote him: "You have made yourself the trustee for those in every country who seek to mend the evils of our condition by reasoned experiment within the framework of the existing social system." In the last months of his life, as the fascist fortress crumbled, it was Roosevelt, far more than Churchill or Stalin, who symbolized liberation for European men and women. To America he bequeathed a precious capital of good will abroad, and to the world the hope of the UN.

He was the most openly human, and fun-lovingest, President since Lincoln. One of his favorite targets was his mother, whom he loved, just as every American boy should, but whom he couldn't resist kidding. When Sara had "important guests" at Hyde Park (back before he was President) he liked to refer to an ancestor on the wall as "that old drunk," or suggest that Claes van Rosenvelt had to leave the Old Country because the law was after him. Sara's gratifying, unfailing response was, "Oh Franklin!" He got a great charge out of a speech to the DAR in which he reminded the ladies that "you and I are descended from immigrants and revolutionaries." He made his tragic affliction a joke, punching Gus Gennerich in the ribs as they maneuvered into and out of the car. Gus and the rest picked up the attitude; when an important call came during a Hyde Park picnic, Gus and a Secret Service agent made a fireman's lift and on the way up to the house Gus started swaying the passenger to the tune of "London Bridge is falling down," which broke up a man crippled by polio.

222

When his valet fell asleep several times, leaving him helpless in the Oval Room at night, he couldn't fire the man, and had Eleanor do it, at the same time getting him a nice job in Treasury. Hearing Sherwood, head of the Office of War Information, explain an absence by a trip to an OWI branch to fire somebody, he was incredulous—"I could never do that," he said.

James Roosevelt, returning from the Philippines, too late for the funeral, was outside Grand Central when a taxi driver recognized him, jumped out of his cab and started telling him how much Jimmy's dad had meant to him. His Park Avenue fare put his head out the window and snapped, "I hired you to drive me, not to talk about that —— Roosevelt!" Jimmy had to restrain the cabbie, tears running down his face, from assaulting the man.

The morning after the news from Warm Springs, Harry Hopkins called Sherwood from Rochester, Minnesota. Hopkins, who had demonstrated that he had guts, whatever Mayo had done to him, talked "with a kind of exaltation." He said, "You and I have got something great we can take with us all the rest of our lives. . . . We know it's true what so many people believed about him and what made them love him. The President never let them down. . . . Oh, he could be exasperating, and he could seem to be temporizing, and delaying, and we'd get all worked up when we thought he was making too many concessions to expediency . . . But in the big things—all of the things that were of real, permanent importance—he never let the people down."

As Harold Ickes said, he was a big man with a little dog. When will America have another man that big?

SUGGESTED READING

Freidel, Frank: *Franklin D. Roosevelt: The Apprenticeship, The Ordeal,* and *The Triumph.* A scholarly three-volume account of Roosevelt's early career, up to the election of 1932.

Schlesinger, Arthur M., Jr.: *The Age of Roosevelt.* A lively and expert three-volume history of the national political scene from 1929 to 1936.

Leuchtenburg, William E.: *Franklin D. Roosevelt and the New Deal.* A compact and readable distillation of an enormous amount of primary material, well annotated.

Tugwell, Guy Rexford: *The Democratic Roosevelt* and *The Brains Trust.* First-person recollections and retrospective analyses by a brilliant surviving New Dealer.

Perkins, Frances: *The Roosevelt I Knew.* Oddly organized (topical, not chronological), this book by the first woman cabinet member is wise, sympathetic, not uncritical, and—unlike some of her colleagues' memoirs—modest.

Roosevelt, Eleanor: *This Is My Story, This I Remember, On My Own,* or the three volumes condensed in one, *The Autobiography of Eleanor Roosevelt.* Stilted, bland, yet lovable, and irreplaceable.

Sherwood, Robert: *Roosevelt and Hopkins.* A Broadway playwright's view of World War II seems wide-eyed today, but the book remains fascinating; primary material from the papers of Roosevelt's most important lieutenant is nowhere else available.

Burns, James MacGregor: *Roosevelt: The Lion and the Fox,* "a political biography," objective, discerning; and its sequel, *Roosevelt: The Soldier of Freedom 1940–1945.*

Roosevelt, Elliott: *As He Saw It.* Invaluable (though perhaps not 100% reliable) eyewitness reportage behind important scenes, especially those with Winston Churchill.

Roosevelt, James, and Shallett, Sidney: *Affectionately, FDR.* Appealing reminiscences.

Rollins, Alfred, Jr.: *Roosevelt and Howe.* Slightly disguised by the title, a biography of Louis Howe, who deserved one this good.

Daniels, Jonathan: *Washington Quadrille.* A leisurely, sophisticated account of the life and times of Lucy Mercer Rutherfurd.

LIST OF PHOTOGRAPHS

Picture Editor: Marjorie E. Zelko

FRANKLIN D. ROOSEVELT

INDEX